Plays: Four

The Dishwasher - 2005
Confessions of a rock 'n' roll star - 2007
Gauguin's Ghost Story - 2009
Tommy Greaves - 2014
Unspoken – 2015

Antony J Stowers

Plays: Four

Tony Stowers

The Dishwasher

'The Dishwasher' in its present form started out as something quite different. Between 1999 – 2001 I'd been spending a lot of time in France and watching 'spectacles de la rue' (grand-scale, street, quantum-theatre that moved in and around its audience in public squares, car parks or stadiums). It was that influence that prompted me to put together a script of my own that borrowed from this style - the ability to offer both a visual and musical feast to family audiences without recourse to words, something that would translate to different cultures. In France I spent three days hammering out a 7-page storyboard/script with the Artistic Director of one such company. Back in the UK, I pitched the script to a big outdoor theatre festival in Scotland and even persuaded The Tiger Lillies to write the score, but it began to slip away because it went beyond my capabilities and I eventually scrapped the project, though I did retain the original script. This version isn't related to that original script and is more in line with what I'm used to doing. I envisaged this version as a one-man show for a small audience in a claustrophobic space and accompanying sparse lighting and sound effects. There is something noble in the character's own personality. He treats his mundane task with respect. He represents the millions of people in this world who oil the machinery and make the cogs turn. If the performance comes across as suffocating, intense or disturbing, then that's the intention. In its French translation the narrative is interweaved with revolutionary songs.

Cast:

THE DISHWASHER, Male or Female

The Dishwasher

1.

(We are in a dark place where lights blink off and on at random or as metallic reflections. The noises of a large, industrial kitchen ebb and flow – the lighting of gas, the burning of the rings, the slamming of oven doors, the chopping of vegetables, the blending of ingredients, the frying of sizzling bacon in hot oil, the clunking of a dumb waiter, the wheeling of trolleys, indecipherable exchange of anger and laughter and shouts. Theses sounds fade and give way to one: a powerful jet of water pummels the base of a deep stainless steel sink, gradually filling it, the subtly changing layers of sounds and finally sudden absence of it telling our ears that it is full. An over head light, raw neon, illuminates THE DISHWASHER below it, sitting on a tubular metal chair.)

THE DISHWASHER: The washing-up liquid's industrial strength and not found on the shelf of the Retail Park Supermarket but in 'Specialist Catering Supplies'. One dollop, at the base, water on, bosh - instant suds!

Hot water surges out. I mean, surges. I know the max distance to turn it, the tap. One revolution it is, one revolution. Anything more than one revolution and it punches the bottom and fountains up all over the place. Anything less and it dribbles and boredom sets in waiting for it to fill. Within that one turn is cold to the left and scalding to the right – the plumbing engineer knows his job very well. A man becomes familiar with things.

For a long time, I didn't know how much the sinks held. Nobody knew. I asked, but nobody seemed to know. So to satisfy my curiosity I filled the sink one day by drawing the water through a one-gallon container. Ten containers it took to fill. Ten. Ten gallons. I mean, that's quite a lot isn't it, ten gallons of fresh water, just to fill one sink? I don't know what that it is litres. I fill my sink three times a day and work six days a week, so that's . . . one hundred and eighty gallons of water a week. And that's just the Washing Sink. I have three sinks: the Soaking Sink, the Washing Sink and the Rinsing Sink. You do the sums.

I've three sinks because I don't just get cutlery and crockery. I also get pans, utensils, machine parts, crockery, cutlery and baking trays, from the ovens, from the kitchen. If the Cooks burn things it's because they know they don't have to wash them. They're paid to cook – not worry about whether or not the pans are clean.

The Washing Sink is where the action is, where it all happens. As a consequence the water becomes dirtier much, much quicker than the water in the Soaking Sink. So I have to replace the water in the Washing Sink more often than I have to replace the water in the Soaking sink and more so than I have to replace the water in the sink to my right, the third sink, the Rinsing Sink, the water in the Rinsing Sink being equivalent to the water in the Soaking sink in that it needs changing not as regularly as the water in the Washing Sink.

The temperature of the water in the Soaking Sink is hot. It needs to be to attack the oils that stick to the bottoms and sides of the pans and the baking trays. The temperature of the water in the Washing Sink however needs to be less hot as I have to work in it and it's where most of the elbow grease is expended. But it doesn't stay hot forever. This is why it needs to be emptied and then refilled again.

Some foolish people think that a large amount of bubbles means the items will clean more quickly and more efficiently, but a large froth of bubbles serves only to reflect the concentrated washing-up liquid in the water's ability to destroy and break down the grease. It is not the consistency of the bubbles but the amount of time they remain in this frothy state that more accurately reflects this, so the bubbles are merely a visible indicator of the effectiveness of the concentrate. When the bubbles begin to diminish, *then* it becomes more difficult to clean your items properly.

The temperature in the Rinsing Sink is moderate, tepid even because it's not there to attack, to undermine stains. It's there to remove excess soap. Remember: the Soaking Sink undermines, the Washing Sink attacks, the Rinsing Sink constitutes. Undermine – Attack – Constitute.

'Where are the dish-washing machines?' I hear you ask. Well now, machines can't replace humans in everything. Humans are unpredictable, especially at feeding time. It's impossible to predict where all the un-eaten, un-served bits are going to end up, nor in what combination they will collect on plates and knives, forks and spoons. You see, it takes considerable hand-pressure to clean a baking tray or a pan caked with congealed fat, considerable hand-pressure. My point is: you can't program a machine to know when to apply considerable hand-pressure at certain points and less hand-pressure at others. A machine's pressure will be constant and all encompassing. Take for example: breakfast cereal, like cornflakes. Cornflakes – relatively few worries but again depending on the amount of sugar either inherent in the constitution of the cornflakes, like frosted flakes or sugar added during the eating by the consumer. But presume the consumer eats flakes free of frosting and doesn't add sugar and you can clean such bowls in seconds. Weetabix however is a nightmare. I swear you can substitute Weetabix for cement – it could hold house bricks in place when it's dried. You can build a wall or a house. My tip: don't let it dry.

Meat always leaves stubborn stains. Well, it's the oil isn't it? Toast doesn't do any damage but jam and marmalade do, the sugar again. Nasty. Butter? No problem, hot water wipes it off with barely a raised eyebrow. But sausages, bacon, eggs, pork, beef, lamb and all related sauces, all these emit a juice, an oil, a natural fatty oil that congeals, dries up, goes black and rock solid. I mean, it's hard to believe we've all got this stuff inside us, seeing how stubborn it is once its squeezed out. I ask the Cooks all the time: 'Why don't you put tinfoil in the base of the grill pans? It'll save so much time, so much energy!' But I get a mouthful of abuse: 'What? You scared of work?'

I like cups - very uniform. Like little boats. Pop them onto the surface of the Washing Sink. They bob around like little ducks. In these big sinks it's possible to create waves. And when you put all these cups in, floating and bobbing around, they contact one another and you hear a gentle percussive one-note symphony of cups, clink-clinking off each other. Clink – clink – clink.

But inevitably the thumb-size handles upset the balance and tips them over to one side and then it just takes one little splash amidst these little waves, a splash of water over the rim and – plop! Down it goes, like the Titanic.

Saucers slide, just slide into the water, like blades, like scimitars, as do dinner plates and side-plates. I take about a dozen dirty dinner plates at a time, stacked on top of each other and lower them straight down into the Soaking Sink, count ten then draw them out one by one from the top of the pile. Left hand draws them out and lowers them halfway into the Washing sink. Right hand wipes one side, wipes the other side. Left hand passes item to right hand. Right hand slides item into Rinsing Sink, where it settles at the bottom in a more random pile.

This leads to displacement. Displacement is, of course, the amount of water displaced by the surface volume of the object pushing against it. It is an ancient theory and something to do with the Ancient Greeks or Sophocles is it or Archimedes?

Cutlery is infinitely trickier but I've a method. I stand a batch of about fifty items of cutlery upright in a specially perforated steel can that sinks to the bottom, like a cylinder-shaped cheese-grater which here when I arrived, so I assume it was invented for this purpose. There's no way around that. Cutlery tends not to pollute the water as much as crockery does. I find that by ignoring the cutlery utensils for about five minutes at a time, the combined friction and motion of the water as I go about the washing of crockery rapidly agitates the dirt affixed to the cutlery, thus loosening it. Although this assists me, it doesn't however omit me from the ultimate responsibility of washing each and every individual item of cutlery by hand to check all stains are removed. That's why I have to change the water in the sinks three times because each time period brings its own problems.

Lunch starts officially at 12 and finishes at 1 but the baking trays and pans arrive from 11.30 as some of the food is passed up to the canteen and distributed on plates and trays in anticipation of the workers queuing at the door. This is the tense period for me – I've got pans and baking trays arriving fresh from the ovens needing to be cleaned and in that critical time period I'm also going to have cutlery and crockery arriving once it has been used by the workers in the canteen, roundabout 12.15 onwards. I've got to be on my toes. Gradually though, the pans and baking trays – the heavy-duty kitchen equipment – will fizzle out and I can switch full-time to crockery and cutlery for the rest of the afternoon.

All this mention of hot water will suggest to you that general overall temperatures in the kitchen must be intense and you'd be right, suffice to say, winter and summer – though obviously more in summer - I sweat like the proverbial pig. It can get almost tropical down here. I shower each night, after work, at home, but I travel home on the train and bus stinking of the kitchen. At home I can cleanse myself of the impurities. It's a ritual.

The baking trays, pots and pans are used at least twice each morning. There aren't enough of them or enough space in the ovens to prepare all food in one go, so the same trays and pans have to be used twice to prepare all the food that will be sold in one go upstairs at lunchtime. The first batch will stay in the restaurant being artificially warmed, waiting for the second batch – still baking – to arrive. Then everything is served together, though the food that's been waiting a while usually gets served first.

This may sound a strange confession to make but I love some of the utensils for their aestheticism, for their form and their easiness to clean. Their form in fact makes them easier to clean. Others, like whisks and grill bars, I hate most of all. I hate whisks. I hate whisks when they get clogged with, say, pancake mixture. You see the problem with whisks is the same problem with grills – the wires are round and fiddly and you have to work all the way around them to be absolutely sure of getting everything off. They require patience whereas my forte is brute force. They're not plain this side or that, they're round. The human brain doesn't work in 3D.

There're lots of machines in the catering industry. Blending machines, whisking machines, tossing machines, peeling machines. Humans are still needed to decide quantity, quality, add ingredients, water, etc but those tasks you'd seen granny do in the good old days no, no, no, forget them. These days: hit a switch and stand back.

The Cooks are only interested in what the machines and ovens produce. They don't give two hoots about the state they leave them in when they've finished. That's beneath them. That's my job. I have to worry about that. And they always want them cleaned urgently, the machines and ovens, so they can do the same thing all over again because there're always more customers coming through the revolving doors.

There are a ready supply of tea towels but rather than drying everything by hand, which I find time-consuming, I generally lay out a bed of drying towels on the worktops behind me and stack all cleaned pots, pans, trays on them, allowing them to drip dry as much as possible before replacing them on shelves, in cupboards or on hooks.

I'm armed with light weaponry: a scouring brush, a Brillo pad and a sponge. They sit next to each other beside the taps. Don't ask me if there's any big mystery to them, like do I favour one over another because it's not so much that I feel compelled to say 'No, I don't' but more like don't make a big thing out of it, you know? There's no mystery.

I have rubber gloves that come up to my elbows because I often have to plunge my arms to the bottom of the sink to retrieve knives, forks, spoons, cups and saucers. The previous dishwasher had rubber gloves that only came over their wrists so these gloves would fill up with water all the time, which kind of defeated the object for me and I could never understand why they didn't do something about it. It showed him up as being mentally deficient in some way I always though. I don't know why this was. Perhaps they lacked vision.

Anyway, once the lunchtime cups have been washed, they're stacked side-by-side on tea trays, each level covered with a dry tea towel until four levels deep. This batch is then put into the service lift and sent up to the top floor where it's stored and re-used the following day.

My Supervisor often praises me on my spotless crockery, cutlery, cooking utensils and clean presentation of my corporate uniform. My Supervisor, who served in the Falklands, assumed for quite some time that I too was ex-services and seemed disappointed to finally learn that I wasn't. I asked him what made him think so. 'Difficulty adjusting,' he said and left it at that, but I have no idea what this means and have never bothered to find out.

And what's this place like, where I work? Well, there're no windows down here in the basement. The walls and floors are tiled blue and the ceiling's painted gloss white. Above the ceiling's the pavement to the street. I know it's the pavement because in the ceiling are those glass bricks. I can't see up pedestrians' trouser legs or skirts or anything – it's all blurred and wavy - nor can I tell if it rains or snows or shines but I do know white is day and black is night.

What am I? Am I a student working my way through college? Am I temping for an agency? Am I an international criminal trying to lay low for a while, or an illegal alien working without fuss at the most mundane job I can find? Am I an itinerant, a vagrant living in a hostel struggling to come to terms with alcoholism? Am I the man who left school with nothing to his name except bad attitude, who washes dishes by day and pretends he's a rock and roll star at night? You decide – while I tell you about the corporation: we drill for oil and gas. And we are a team - of that there is no doubt. We're a multi-national billion-dollar oil company. Our customers are the people of the world who need instant energy to light their lives and cook their meals.

Worldwide we employ twenty thousand but there are about five hundred of us in our building, a large square block filled with rows of small glittering windows. There're twenty floors to the building. The top floor is the restaurant complex. The top floor and basement are connected by means of two hydraulic service lifts – one taking up trays of prepared food and other dishes, the other bringing down cutlery and crockery. All floors between the basement and the top floor are turned over for the exclusive use of the office staff that work for the corporation. I took plastic cups up to the vending machine on the eighth recently and had to ask a lady, a secretary I think, where the vending machine was. I remember thanking her. I remember the way she looked at me. I remember her white teeth and perfume. I remember the light behind her.

Humans are aliens. To each other I mean, we're aliens. I'm almost ninety-nine per cent sure we look at each other and think: 'They know something about this world that I don't know.' For example, an ugly person thinks a beautiful person knows something they don't know and a beautiful person thinks an ugly person knows something they don't know and so on. We all mistakenly think that other people hold keys to doors we cannot open for ourselves, so we wait in vain for others to open the doors to wisdom and enlightenment. And when the doors fall open, we just expect the product we've been seeking to emerge wrapped and packaged for our consumption. But it's a lie – we're all product. Some of us suss this quickly and do something about it before its too late. But millions never get it and die in ignorance.

See? See what you get when you stick an intelligent brain into an unskilled job? Kitchen sink philosophy!

I clean the objects that make the food that feed the people who make the orders that move the units around the world. It's as simple as that. And yes there are days when I feel proud, very proud and very safe. Then there are other times, like today, I turn to lay a newly washed pan on the draining board, like so. I move my feet, I dance, like so. Right foot first, left foot to follow up to the instep of the right, then back in reverse order to face the sink, to begin the process all over again. Then it whacks me like a bolt from the blue!

(The startling noise of a large glass jug breaking on a tiled floor hits out ears)

We're all slaves in bondage and Hell is mindless, repetitive, numbing tasks to occupy the waking hours. Here we go, hoarding our saved time, repeating ourselves, frantically seeking a magical memory labelled 'Forever Elusive', a moment to grab and call our own, where we can say: 'Stop! This is it! This is the moment of bliss I've worked towards and sacrificed everything for! Hold the clock! This is it!' But of course the clock doesn't stop and nobody else seems to notice.

(We hear the noise of water gurgling down a plughole)

I squirt the washing-up liquid around the sides and rub off the scum and grease with a soft sponge until everything shines. I unblock the plugholes of their lumps of gristle and slime by sticking my fingers in, lifting it out and flicking it into a bin so the last of the water can run freely down into the sewer.

You know, you're wrong to assume the world of the lowly dishwasher is without worth, without value. The dishwasher, it could be argued, is the lintel that holds up the building, the most vital block in the foundations, keeping spotless and ready-for-action the tools that feed the army. Should he threaten to remove that block then those above him must either replace him or resign themselves to an inevitable catastrophe that will unravel like knots threads in a safety net.

I've met my Nemesis. I've seen it in the endless rivers of pots and pans, cups and saucers, knives and forks that flow around and around the kitchen. And the things that come out of the kitchen flow around and around the building. And the people who occupy the building go around and around the world. Used and re-used, scrubbed and scalded, washed and wiped, dipped and dried, placed and polished, over and over and over again.

They'll scrub me out one day and I'll be replaced.

One dollop, at the base, water on, bosh - instant suds! Hot water surges out. I mean, surges. Of course I know the max distance to turn it, the tap. One revolution it is. One revolution. Anything more than one revolution and it punches the bottom of the sink and fountains up. Anything less and it dribbles and boredom sets in as one waits for it to fill. A man becomes familiar with things.

They'll scrub me out one day. Oh I know they will, I know they will, they'll scrub me out. We all get scrubbed out. We're all dirty dishes.

(The neon light above him flickers. He looks up. It goes out and stays out. End)

Confessions of a rock n roll star

'Confessions' started life as a short story I wrote in 1996 when living in the North East of England and was lamenting (or fantasising) on a celebrity career that passed me by. I'm sure millions around the world frequently strike up poses with tennis racquets and sweeping brushes in the form of guitars and escape the drudge of their daily lives by imitating legendary rock stars from time to time and I'm certain I'm not alone; many people I know dedicated their entire lives to living like a rock star despite clearly not being one.

In 1997 I read it as part of a show of other readings and it got a few laughs and then I stored it away for ten years until moving to France in 2006 and translating it into French in 2008. It was first performed in Angers, France in December 2008. Juan Requejo was the 'ROCKSTAR'. We reworked the show and it was performed again in The Jam Club in March 2009. Both shows featured music by Led Zeppelin, Jimi Hendrix, The Doors, Pink Floyd, Dire Straits, Iggy Pop, The Sex Pistols and The Rolling Stones.

I see this performance as more than just a microscopic examination of frustrated ambition but also a celebration of cultural touchstones - rock music tracks that help take us out of whatever daily miseries we often find ourselves entangled in. I don't want the music tracks playing little more than a supporting role to the action, brief interludes connecting ideas; these songs are classic songs and mean a great deal to a great deal of people and I'd like them included in carefully controlled lengths, to be considered as important as the words and action. Any actor playing this role must be very familiar with the tracks and how they are structured so that they can co-ordinate their own actions and words.

Cast:
ROCKSTAR, 40-50

Confessions of a rock n roll star

1.

(ROCKSTAR stands with his back to the audience wearing only his underpants. A guitar strap runs across his back, appearing to be strapped to – presumably - a guitar we can't quite see. The lights illuminate him as they would a rock star live in concert – even though it's clear he's in a cramped room without windows: an old armchair and ironing board on each side hemming him in. Against the armchair is a cheap, battered toy acoustic guitar with only three strings. A shelf along the back wall holds a few books like 'No One Here Gets Out Alive' and various music books and there's also a table on which is a small fridge, a Microwave oven and a one-ring electric cooker with a simple wooden chair with a worn seat beside it. Another cupboard shelf contains some plates, crockery, cups, pans and a few tins of beans and vegetables. There is an old gas fire on the back wall with two speakers either side on the floor. Around the gas fire is a mantelpiece on which is a stereo CD player and a vertical CD rack, as well as framed photographs. A faded red carpet covers the floor with a few porno magazines scattered near the armchair. A leather jacket, some t-shirts and jeans hang from hangers on a coat-rack. Posters of rock icons Robert Plant (Led Zeppelin), Jim Morrison, Jimi Hendrix, the Rolling Stones, The Sex Pistols and Mark Knopfler adorn the walls. All in all, ROCKSTAR lives in a cramped, gloomy bed-sitter. The lights come up to Dire Straits intro for 'Money for Nothing' and, just as the famous guitar riff kicks in, ROCK STAR turns to his audience – us – to reveal, attached to the guitar strap, a battered plastic toy acoustic with only five strings - for the first verse and one chorus. His miming includes various poses associated with rock guitarists as well as miming to the words. The track cuts out abruptly.)

ROCKSTAR: 'My first guitar?' My God, it seems so long . . .

(He takes off the toy acoustic and stands it against the table leg and then sits on the armchair and takes up the real battered acoustic and strums once)

My Uncle Elvis - Elvis Bartholomew – ageing Teddy Boy, Brylcreem and sideburns - bought me my first guitar for my eighth birthday. Well, it was that or horse-riding lessons. I learned (sings and plays badly with great labour and discord)

'Twinkle, twinkle, little star, how I wonder what you are. Up above the sky so bright, like a diamond in the night. Twinkle, twinkle, little star, how I wonder what you are.'

And gave up.

(He steps to the table and takes a tin of Ravioli and opens it with a tin opener)

Years later, many years later, I tried again. I'd just finished reading Eric Burdon's autobiography so found myself a collar-up, heel-clicking strut and strode shit-hot confident into a guitar shop in Kilburn High Street, London, got me a white six-string Marlin acoustic and paid with a cheque that bounced all over town. I went to another store in Bond Street, shoplifted me a book of Doors songs, took the both home to my student flat in east London, learned three chords, strummed them fuckers to death, posed in front of the mirror and swapped the guitar for a packet of johnnies and an eighth of hash. And I never did learn to ride a horse nor play the guitar.

(The tin open, he eats direct from it with a fork)

I played drums – once. Do you know the intro to Cozy Powell's 'Dance with the Devil'? Neither did my neighbours. I tried singing. Me and a mate recorded a song on a cheap tape recorder. We called it 'The Offence', after one of the few films Sean Connery did where he was a real actor, and it lived up to its name that song. If nothing else, it was a capital crime against music. It took thirty minutes to write, ten minutes to record and we never did think of a name for our group.

(Cue: The Doors' 'Light my Fire' comes to life. The tin of Ravioli half-finished, he leaves it and steps up to the ironing board. As the song progresses, he irons his denim Jeannes. They are faded with the customary rip in the left knee. At one time the iron becomes his microphone and the ironing board becomes Ray Manzarek's keyboard, so the song continues until the first half of that keyboard solo before Robby Kreiger's guitar picks up the tune.)

ROCKSTAR: Yeah, man, my life as a rock n roll star was unique – in that I never climbed up onto a stage in front of ten thousand screaming fans, a bottle of vodka kicking the piss out of my liver and half of Peru up my nose to shout: 'This is not a rebel song!' before picking up my credit cards and being chauffeured to a wrecked hotel room. Nor did I live as a recluse in a Scottish castle, attracting twice as much attention by publicly shunning the limelight, condemned to composing concept albums with sleeve notes designed by Roger Dean, Gerald Scarfe and Rene Magritte.

(He pulls his Jeans on. It's not easy to fasten them around the middle – he has to breathe in. He opens the door of his small fridge and takes out a can of beer he drinks from.)

ROCKSTAR: My career began in the 1970's in secondary school. Collector's favourites like Led Zep two, three and four, Cheap Trick Live at the Budokan, The Wall, Sabbath Bloody Sabbath, Master of the Universe and If You Want Blood swapped sweaty palms in science class, smuggled home in grubby satchels along with French homework exercise books where the scratches would be listened to and added to on cheap and nasty record players and where our fresh young minds would adjust to the craft of the rock n roll star. Their words inspired us to reach for the moment, to live in the now, to rebel against authority, to fuck the system our teachers represented, to talk back and fight back. The rock stars were our poets, our bards, our cheap operatic philosophers and the warriors of our teenage wasteland. Rock stars lifted us up to dizzy, breathtaking heights and then our parents brought us back down to earth again with 'TURN THAT BLOODY RUBBISH DOWN!'

(The Sex Pistols 'Anarchy in the UK' plays. He picks up his first cowboy boot and starts polishing it, occasionally slipping into the track with a gesture or a grimace. It covers the background just enough for him to be audible above it.)

ROCKSTAR: Then we tasted our punk years – the Pistols, the Clash, Blondie, The Stranglers, The Skids, Stiff Little Fingers and The Jam. Suddenly working class politics was back on the menu having disappeared up its own arse after the Sixties with 'prog-rock'. We cut our hair shorter and shorter as gestures of revolt though our attitudes stayed the same. So many names, so many songs, so many words, musicians and producers, so may hopes and dreams, a new wave that eventually crashed against the shore and the tide turned in February '79 when Sid OD'd.

(He continues to polish and 'play' until the guitar riff of the song. He finds a box of cigarettes but it is empty so he takes dog ends out of the ashtray and rolls the stubs into a cigarette paper to roll one frail and flimsy cigarette. With some relief and pride he puts it between his lips. The song finishes. Rockstar tries to light his 'rollie' but discovers his lighter is out of gas.)

ROCKSTAR: But we didn't want to die. Not like that. Not like Sid or Jim or Jimi, Janis or Ian. It was okay for them to die, but not us. We weren't them. They were stars – they were on the telly, in the papers. We were nowhere: working class kids in school uniforms, mincemeat, fodder, minnows in the river, flies around shit. We only dreamed of pushing the envelope, of going to the edge; we could pull back when our Mam's banged on our bedroom doors and shouted 'Put that bloody light out!' We were spotty, snot-nosed teenagers whose highlight of the week was Top of the Pops and jerking off to posters of Debbie Harry and Bo Derek hanging on walls of paisley wallpaper.

(He picks up the sweeping brush and holds it upside down as if it is a guitar)

Instead, thanks to Joe Strummer and Pete Townsend, I awoke to the poses of the guitarist slashing at the strings, arms rolling round and round like the sails of a windmill or shimmying down a microphone rope, eyes rolling up to heaven, too fucked-up to focus, amplifying grunts and groans, lapping up wave after wave of adoration and applause, sweeping brush slung low and mean across my groin and a punch to the sky. Rock stars were our priests, their songs their sermons, their concerts our holy masses and our cries our adoration.

(He flicks through a well-thumbed copy of 'No One here Gets Out Alive')

Rock n roll stars ruled the world and sold mountains of records, too quickly gleaning the fruits of their labours, took overdoses and cried out for help to cope with their sudden meteoric rises, drove Limousines into lamp posts, lived in California in their heads and in their beds, New York Warhol-ian warehouses or tax-free havens where only the locals knew their names.

Rock n roll stars retired, took sabbaticals with enlightened but expensive gurus and then re-appeared in tattoos and leather guarded by evil-looking celebrity gangsters.

Rock n roll stars criticised singers who mimed their songs and accused them of selling out – and then did the same themselves a few years later with a shrug of 'If you can't beat 'em . . . '

(He picks up one of his porno magazines and the centrefold falls out)

And when they married, they married dumb blonde Page 3 tarts barely out of school and made the front covers of tabloids with their long hair tumbling down incongruously over their shoulders.

(He throws the magazine back from where it came and turns)

And then they divorced.

(He turns back and has another quick glance at one particular image)

And after a few weeks re-married again.

Rock n roll stars mocked all conventions and we egged them on, daring them to jump so we could watch the spectacle but they could pay the price.

(Jimi Hendrix 'Red House' plays. ROCKSTAR begins polishing his second boot, as before, taking moments out to 'feel' the music with a gesture or a grimace. He then uses his boot as a reporting journalist might use a microphone to interview strangers in the street, imitating the voice of Alan Whicker, a once-well-known interviewer with a distinctive vocal style, for each of the following questions.)

But what were they really like, behind the image? What music did they like? What did they eat for breakfast? What film stars did they admire? Whose shirts did they wear? Which brand of cigarettes did they smoke? Where did they buy their socks? What did they think of politics? Who were their influences? What brand of toilet paper did they use? Did they believe in God? Did they love their Mums? What car did they drive? What did they think of other pop stars? Who did they hang out with? What beer did they drink? Who cut their hair? Where did they go to school? What pets did they have and what were their names? What was their favourite colour? Who was their favourite group? What did they think of the current number one? Did they give to charity? Who did they vote for? What shampoo did they wash their hair with? What toothpaste did they brush their teeth with? How old was their car? Who did they bank with? What newspapers did they read? What books? Where did they holiday? Who was that mystery girl other than their regular wife or partner they went to the nightclub with last night? Who was that mystery guy? Were they gay? Had they experimented? Did they take drugs? What drugs had they taken? Had they ever broken the law? Didn't they have more important things to do than answer stupid questions?

(He pulls on his left boot)

Rock n roll stars fed us every morsel, every titbit, and how we hung on their every word, their every syllable, savouring the paradox of brushing the hem of their kaftans to discover their fragility. They were living proof that a man's education and background could be rooted in soil as insignificant as our own. How could we imagine them growing up and kicking cans in back alleys of towns as shit-sounding as Stoke-on-Trent, Leeds, Newcastle or Darlington, whistling Elvis songs or Beatles tunes, going to shit schools, not standing out, uniform, dull, as mundane as us? No, no, it could never be. There had to be a way out and they had to have the key.

(He pulls on his right boot)

Rock n roll stars were generally from poorly educated, staunch Labour-voting working class families born in council houses and, once rich and famous, sent their kids to Eton and Oxford University and voted Tory, brushing shoulders with top-flight accountants who would cook tomorrow's books, lawyers who would weasel them out of scrapes and judges who would let them off charges of illegal drug-taking or speeding in built-up areas. How could we compare their power and influence with us with our second-hand cars, greasy fry-ups, synthetic leather and nylon-cushioned sofas, apprenticeships in welding and weeklong catering holidays in Blackpool?

(He stands. Led Zeppelin's 'Whole Lotta Love' plays. He takes a black leather bike jacket from the rack but instead of putting it on, studies it. As the instrumental portion of the track arrives, he talks)

ROCKSTAR: We were masochists. What masochists we were – emptying our pockets to line theirs, to reinforce their excess. We used them, egged them on to daring new heights of danger, sacrifice, degradation, public humiliation and in return they fleeced us for every cent we had. They cast their shadows and we walked in them. Second best was an ocean of vinyl, forests of posters, a daily deluge of reviews and articles and gossip in national and international magazines, shoe shops that sold chunky, buckled boots, fashion boutiques that sprung up and disappeared overnight like late winter daffodils and sold beads, bangles, silver crosses on silver chains, hoops and skull-rings, earrings and studs, patches and badges, t-shirts and tea towels, hair dyes, patchouli oil, sunglasses for cloudy days, fur-lined leathers for heat wave days, flaunting our rebelliousness on the last bus home or listening to 'Purple Haze' on the Radiogram.

(He lets the leather jacket drop to the floor. The track fades and he looks about him, listening to the silence, searching for an elusive word)

With my incapacity to concentrate for a long enough time to string together more than three chords on a guitar, two verses and one chorus with an instrumental break, life became one long guitar solo. I couldn't hold a regular beat on a drum as I couldn't hold a regular beat on anything else – jobs, education, women and I'd a singing voice like a cat with a tuning fork shoved up its arse. For me, it was always tomorrow, tomorrow, but for thirty years tomorrow never came and then suddenly it was there and it'd turned into yesterday.

(He moves to the walls and very slowly runs his fingers over the posters of his rock star heroes, his face touching the posters as if listening to them speak or kissing them)

Where did it all go wrong? Where did it all go right? Jimi, Jim – did it hurt? Is it like closing your eyes and going to sleep? Or is there a sharp, a too sharp, a painful, painful sensation? Is it like switching off the power? Sid – was it worth it?

I was so shit at school. I mean, I could have . . . but it was easier to run. Easier to run and hide. Pretend. I pretended. In my imaginary world were worlds of dreams and worlds of possibilities. I slipped shining out of school stupid and terrified, like a baby born standing up and worked endless, mundane jobs, temporary, contracted, commission-based, targets, incentives, goals, gambling, prizes, rewards, carrots, temptations. Always around the corner, it was always just around the corner. Dignity subjected under the Cuban heel of my own freewill to fuel the desire to strut upon the catwalk of Zap City. Friday and Saturday night became the new Sunday. My life is a 'join-the-dots' of weekends with rope bridges in between. Holy nights. Sacred nights. The twin peaks of rock n roll nightlife. See me. Remember me? Leather jeans, fuck off boots, slicked back hair, ears buzzing with a tousled guitar fuzz, going halves on drugs and drink, staggering home eating chips, pissing in telephone boxes, dreaming up songs that came to nothing. Remember me? Remember me – it's a statement not a question.

('Another Brick in the Wall Part 2' by Pink Floyd plays. As it plays, he continues to feel his way around the wall as if trying to detect a voice beyond. As the famous guitar solo clicks in, he picks up his tennis racquet once again and, though miming, takes us through one of the most low-key and convincing 'air guitar' mimes ever seen. It is almost beautiful to watch. The track stops at four minutes with the ringing of a phone. He looks at his own 'phone and picks it up.)

ROCKSTAR: Hello? Hello? Is there anybody . . . out there?

(He hangs up)

We derided discipline. Rock n roll stars didn't need discipline! They pleased themselves. They didn't need

31

no fucking education to guarantee success. We all knew how most adults turned out after a lifetime sucking up to the system – they wore corduroy jackets, loafers, shirts and ties. They married young and died old, clapped out, fucked up, sucked dry by grasping kids. Their mortgages were life sentences. We saw no glamour in chalk dust and theory. Better, we thought, to explode in brief but beautiful, breath-taking glory like a firework rocket than hang in endless space like a burnt out planet or a gaping cavity that once bore a rotten tooth.

(He fondly handles the photographs on his mantle)

ROCKSTAR: Oh my adorable Annie, my sweet Susannah, my lovely lady Eleanor, happy Helen, crazy Karen, sexy Sarah – will you ever forgive me? I was young. I was stupid. I was blind. I was cruel and obsessed. Forgive me, for the hurt I put on you. Your vengeance is complete – look at me now: nothing, without children, alone, trapped, poor, scraping by, death on two legs. I deserve it. Don't I deserve it? I fucked my life. I fucked up all that was beautiful and for what - for a dream, for a fantasy. Take a message to the young of today: don't do it, don't go there. Rock n roll is on the edge of your world, not in the centre. Embrace the simplicity – be happy with what you can do in school and don't be sad if you cannot be what others want you to be, for you're unique. Work the shittiest jobs you can so you can learn how to aim for the better ones. Learn self-respect and pride. Be content to get up early and go to bed late after a hard day at work. Don't smoke, don't take drugs and drink in moderation. Drugs change nothing. They only delay what must be inevitably faced. Love your mother and father and, though their heroes may be older and their dress and manners clumsy don't forget how they were young once too and went through the same painful routine of self-awareness. Keep your seed pure and wholesome and love your children. Teach them to respect others and themselves, to do well at school, to eat up their greens, not to be cheeky, to take their exams and vote with their consciences, to respect other races and not judge men by the colours of their skin but the contents of their characters. Obey the law and pay your taxes. Always be honest and trust that your neighbour as is as honest as you and cares as much about living in a safe society.

(He sobs, collapsing to the floor. 'It's Only Rock n Roll' by the Rolling Stones begins to play quietly in the background. He stays there for some minutes gradually leaving his sobs behind and slowly transforming them into a barely audible titter of amusement and, eventually, a raucous laughter as the music builds.)

ROCKSTAR: And kiss my arse. And jump in a lake. And stand on your head. And fuck off out of it. Me, I'm a rock n roll star, you mothers - old? No doubt! Set in my ways? For sure! Living in the past? That's me! Immature and ridiculous, the oldest teenager in the business? I'll name that tune in one! But I'll never sell my villa in Spain or auction my gold discs or donate my collection of invisible Rickenbackers and Les Paul's to charity. And I'll never compromise 'cause I've got jack shit to compromise, Jack. Unless, the taxman comes a-knocking and it's time to release my greatest hits.

(The track cuts out on: 'But I like it, like it, yes I do' Lights to black)

(End)

Gauguin's Ghost Story – 2009

I started writing my Gauguin story in 2003 when I lived in North East England. I suspected at the time it would be one of the most ambitious projects I'd ever tackled simply because it was above and beyond my usual fare and I felt hard-pushed to find an audience for it in what was then my native stomping ground of North East England. Much regional theatre in those days was only supported if the themes of the work were related to the region or its heritage. Perhaps that's still the case today.So I 'put it to bed' for a while and then a couple of years later found myself living in France, so drove up to Pont-Aven in Brittany in January 2008 and started working on the 're-vamp' from that day forward until the summer of 2009 when I first performed it there. The script changed a lot over 18 months as I adapted some paragraphs from English to French, the new version being bi-lingual.This is the original English version I wrote in France but then changed to suit French audiences. A Geordie accent would be mostly meaningless to French ears. As for previous plays, I've often written one-man shows purely for budgetary reasons, but I see no great problems with the play being performed by numerous actors (the characters are clearly marked) in an ensemble-type performance. To immediately deflect accusations that I 'don't have much of a story', I'm not interested in that. What I always aimed for in this piece is to be so fluent with the lines that it's the spontaneous-ness of the performance that brings it to life. The idea is that the actor(s) is/are 'visited' by Gauguin's ghost for the duration of the performance and that hopefully no two performances will be identical.In this current English form it's never been performed but in the French bilingual version it was performed in 2009 in Pont-Aven in August, Paris in September and Angers in November. I then changed the set and reworked the show, creating a one square metre canvas collage of images from Gauguin's life, his work and the work of many of his contemporaries as the main prop and decided to perform in art galleries rather than in theatres. It played again the following year in galleries in Paris in October 2010 and again in May and June 2011. I've marked characters' speaking roles but purely as mimicked voices and personalities to be created by the actor.

Gauguin's Ghost Story

1.

(Onstage is one large collage of images from Gauguin and his life. It hangs amongst whatever other works are on display in the gallery at that time, or it dominates the 'gallery' space. It is to this collage that the actor traces certain images to which he refers as the piece progresses. Gauguin is a member of the audience invited to view the exhibition. He must – as the other characters should they be involved – be dressed in contemporary fashions and appear to be 'the same as everyone else'. Actors should adapt their speech to whatever accent suits them best. In this case: Geordie/North east England.)

GAUGUIN: 'What shall we do with a drunken painter? What shall we do with a drunken painter? What shall we do with a drunken painter earl-y in the morning?' The things these eyes have seen, the places, the people... Why? What was it all for? Six years in the Navy - stoking the boilers mind you, not poncing it as Petty Officer in white shirt with gold-braid – taught me everything I know. I learned to cook, to drink, to put it about, to fight, how I fought - and fucked! But I've found nowt on land that replaces the freedom of the sea, nowt - not even painting, I swear down!

'So, Monsieur Gauguin, tell us about your life.'

I thought you'd never ask, pet. Me life I lived as I chose, mate: I said please and thank you, bowed for ladies, shook hands with men, kept me dignity, shared what little I had. But it wasn't enough. It never will be. Why?

Because I know what you say about me. You say: 'Gauguin? Isn't he the one who dumped his wife and kids to gan to Tahiti and chase lasses in hula-hoop skirts?'

Well, it wasn't *quite* like that but then nowt ever is, is it?

Rewind time: what's ten years? Most of us can picture ten years. Now multiply it by 16. Nah, I was shite at Maths an' all. But it don't seem so long ago does it? Peru, I just about remember Peru. 1849, the French *coup d'etat,* Napoleon III, just after. Me parents ran, I was so big (he indicates a small baby)… relatives there, Peru… *en route* Dad's ticker (he indicates his chest exploding) … in Peru, me Uncle Don Pio took us to a bullfight for me seventh birthday. . . gives us a dead bull's ear as a trophy… the passion of South America, man… four years in exile and when I gets back to France, an accent like a Peruvian donkey! Bishop Dupanloup, high school in Orleans:

DUPANLOUP (French accent): So, young Eugene Henri, tell me: vat do you vant to be ven you grow up?

GAUGUIN: I'd settle for being a living legend, Father Dupanloup.

DUPANLOUP: A living legend? Did you hear zat, Lord? Eugene Henri, half of you's tame and half of you is vild. I blame your childhood. Peruvians are savages: cannibalism, human sacrifice, idol worship. Zis is France, not Peru. Here we write ze rules of civilization, zere zey test them. How can you hope to get good qualifications witzzout French, all day long drawing and sketching and no father of your own to whip you into

38

shape? What's zat, Lord? Yes, I zink you're right. You must go on studying your Bible – you're at least good at zat - but I must give you two with ze stick for your audacity!

GAUGUIN: Whey-aye, Father. Mucho-grassy-ass, Father. When me Mam died I was sad of course but not too sad: her spirit of independence passed into me, but independence is nowt without contacts. Enter 'Uncle' Gustave. An 'uncle' is what you call your Mam's bit-on-the-side when your real Dad scarpers.

GUSTAVE (Yorkshire accent): Before yer Ma died I promised, as yer guardian, to tak care o' yer, so I've found yer a job. Yer t'start at Bertin's as'r *liquidateur.* Outside of t'Official Stock Exchange is a second group o' traders called *coulissiers.* They stabilize share prices, which is a good thing for countries like ours wrecked by t'Prussians, trying to rebuild Paris. You settle up t'dealings 'twixt the *coulissiers* and t'shareholders on time and in full. 'Am I qualified for such a job, Uncle?' yer ask. Six years at sea *and* yer saw action? Yer've broad shoulders, lad – and yer'll need 'em - sound credentials for t'art o' persuasion. It's well paid – mostly commission - and dull as ditchwater but fret not - all my life I worked dull, stupid jobs as'r means to an end. Yer can start Mundee. Meanwhile, some new paintings 'ave arrived. Art and culture in this day and age is revolution Paul - buying it's t'act of a sub-ver-sive. I must do summat wi' me brass and art excites us as I'm too old to man barricades or plant black flags. Camille Pissarro, a four-by-two, is coming for tea wit'h is friend Claude Monet. A new style of painting's emerging, did yer know? We shall have t'think of a name for this new style for it's leaving an impression.

GAUGUIN: and then the hands of the Impressionists themselves - a tag foisted on them by a Parisian reviewer - blessed me. I met: Monet, Manet, Cezanne, Sisley, Renoir and Degas. The approval of Degas meant the most, like - he taught wuh about the use of memory.

(He indicates 'Self Portait' by Edgar Degas.)

DEGAS (RP): Marvellous. We invite you to exhibit a painting in the Fourth Impressionist Exhibition and you submit a piece of sculpture. Gauguin, you're determined to stand out and I admire that. But be careful, don't push your luck, not with me, for I despise the term 'Impressionism' and I hate gangs. In fact, I hate gangs almost as much as I hate the working class and I hate the working class almost as much as I hate Jews.

GAUGUIN: Aw hey, that's not very PC that, Edgar mate. Me teacher - Divvent-tek-the-Pissarro - says you're a pain in some ways, but frank and loyal in others.

DEGAS: Divvent-tek-the-Pissarro? Don't assume that 'cause a man likes your work, he also likes you.

GAUGUIN: I'll make a note of that the next time you show interest in one of me pieces, Monsieur Degas.

DEGAS: Look Gauguin, it's all very well to copy what one sees, but it's much better to draw what one remembers. Imagination links with memory. Reproduce only what's striking, which is to say only what's necessary. Thus, your memories and fantasies are liberated from the tyranny of Nature.

GAUGUIN: Wise words. He snubbed wuh many times in the beginning did Degas, cantankerous auld scrote. He wasn't the only one: many people snubbed wuh, not only 'cause I was stubborn but also 'cause I was untrained. True, I was isolated and lonely but I produced. I did produce. I was very productive. And very reproductive: me long-suffering wife: Mette. They say men often marry their Mams but in my case I seem to have married me Granny. Me real granny was Flora Tristan, The Worker's Saint - a radical feminist and socialist beacon. I married a Danish pastry: Mette Gad from Copenhagen.

(He indicates 'Mette Gad' – a side view of her in a strapless dress on a chair.)

All she wanted was a rich husband and an account at the best pie shop in town. Instead she got five bairns - and me.

METTE (Danish accent): I don't understand, Paul. Why must we move to a poorer part of Paris? I'm happy here. And why do we rarely go to the theatre or the opera? You spend all your spare time painting or mixing with your artist friends in cafes and restaurants. I never see you. I gave up the dullness of Copenhagen for life with you in gay Paris, but not this life. What about our children?

GAUGUIN: Sorry pet, bit pre-occ'd. Whose work to see next and why? So I could learn from them! They were the Masters, they'd trained at the Academy, who else could teach wuh?

METTE: What did I just say, Paul?

41

GAUGUIN: I divvent kna, pet, what did you just say? Who cares eh? Too wrapped up in me own world with thoughts of which painting to submit to the exhibition at the Salon in 1876. I thought mebbes 'The Seine at the Pont D'Iena'?

(He indicates the painting)

Queued for hours in a line that stretched around four buildings and then we all passed in front of the judges like railway carriages in a station. They sky-ed us, up near the ceiling, but it was a start. Copied straight from the style of Jongkind and Corot, they said. That's what pleased the judges from The Salon – Plebs! But it's not a question of copying, man. It's a question of experiencing as much as you can and from that pile o' shite identifying the missing link. That missing link becomes your own style, the next generation.

And as for marriage: for the record, *Mette - left – me*, I didn't leave Mette. In '79 I made 30,000 francs from the Market! We were rollin' in it, man! How could she not have been happy with that? Oh she was happy, so happy she spent it as fast as I made it.

Okay, it wasn't exactly like that – in '84 we went to Copenhagen and I organised an exhibition of me work, but after five days it was closed down by the Danish Academy. 'Bugger off!' they says. 'I want to go back to Paris' I tells the wife. 'Bugger off then!' she says, 'Bugger off' says her family and 'Bugger off!' says every-bugger.

That was me painful apprenticeship.

'It's not my problem!' – that's the slogan between artists these days. Example, in '81, I met Cezanne: what did you mean, Monsieur Cezanne, when you said that you thought Impressionism was smouldering and some new form was being created from its ashes?

'I cannot stop you looking at my work, Gauguin, but you will not have the key to my soul,' 'e says, all arty-farty like. He was paranoid we all wanted to steal from him but only thieves steal.

In '73 Monet caused a sensation with a picture of a reclining nude called 'Olympia'. I 'borrowed' from that for one of me own, a parody if you like, a nude sewing, that went into the 6th Exhibition in '81.

(He mounts 'Study of a Nude – Suzanne Sewing')

I *knew* I was onto summat when a critic called Huysmans praised me effort: 'Monsieur Gauguin is the first artist in years to have attempted to represent the woman of today'

Glory! Marvellous innit? It's like absinthe: a super head-change for a short time and after that it falls, little by little, into the banal reality. And it doesn't pay the rent. How long was it, three years? Got a job as a billposter on five francs a day, starved, weight plummeted, shoes and clothes like holes sewn together. But I kept on painting. I always believed me fortune'd change and I'd get back with me wife and children and be a good father. Aye an' pigs might fly.

When the 8th Impressionist Exhibition come along, I was asked to display summat but George Seurat stole the show -.
(He traces 'A Sunday Afternoon on the island of Grandes Jatte'- by Georges Seurat)

- short strokes of pure colour laid side-by-side to leave the eye to mix them. Trip City! How did it come about, Georges?

SEURAT (RP): What do you most f-f-f-f-fear, Gauguin?

GAUGUIN: Most, George? What me Impressionist peers will think of us if I tell them I wanna work more in the studio than in the open air. I'm fretted the'll tak the piss, man.

SEURAT: Then embrace your f-f-f-f-f-fear, Paul. Chances are others will f-f-f-f-fear it too. F-f-f-f-fear commands respect. Or they'll laugh. But don't f-f-f-f-f-orget: laughter is often an expression of f-f-f-f-fear.

GAUGUIN: You sound so... well f-f-f-f-fed, George.

SEURAT: My f-f-f-f-f-father indulges me. Money buys security, security buys time, time buys luxury to experiment. But you'll f-f-f-f-find neither time nor security in Paris. Try Pont Aven, Brittany. I've heard there's an innkeeper who trades paintings f-f-f-f-f-or a bed and meals.

GAUGUIN: Ah, Pont Aven, Pont Aven, the Whitley Bay of Brittany... Hotel Gloanec, run by the able-bodied Madame Gloanec...

MADAME GLOANEC (London accent): Fish and chips and a straw mattress, Monsieur Gauguin.

GAUGUIN: Are yer haven a laugh there Mrs G?

GLOANEC: Lucky for you, Mr Gauguin!

GAUGUIN: Who else's come for the summer, Madame?

GLOANEC: Let me see, we have a Dutchman: Jacob Meyer De Haan – a most curious specimen if ever I saw one...

(He taps his own 'Meyer De Hann' portrait)

DE HAAN (Dutch accent): I'm reading zis book, Paul. It's called 'Ze Tailor Retailored' in English, Thomas Carlyle: 'Clozes: zeir origin und influence'. It's not about clozes literally of course, clozes is ze metaphor for culture, zrowing off ze old vays of zinking und replacing zem wiz new: a process constant of ze death und ze rebirth. You know you really ought to learn ze English. I'm staying at a farm at Le Pouldu, a village a kilometres from here. I've rented a studio. It's private – no tourists. You should come und stay.

GAUGUIN: Und I did... und togezzer we got pissed az ratz und painted ze interiors of ze dining room of ze hotel of Marie Henry, much to ze delight of ze locals.

De Haan reminded wuh of an intelligent demon - he had a face like a dog's bum with a hat on but he was sharp as a razor, so sharp I put his ugly face in some of me work and used his ideas almost immediately - Symbolism they called it – 'Freudian Abstract' they might call it today

'Arty-fart Shite' they'd call it doon the boozah. Parisian reviewers also happened to champion Symbolism and recognised their ideas in me new works and give us good reviews. Whey-aye, course, it was political, but not short sighted - all me work retained this central theme after. Who else, Madame Gloanec?

GLOANEC: There's Monsieur Emile Bernard...

BERNARD (Scottish accent): I've heard a rumour that you're claiming to be the inventor of Symbolism in art, hen? I hope it's not true. You know that it was me who first covered this area. Be warned, Gauguin: history will vindicate me, d'yer ken? Meanwhile, I've mail, from another mad Dutchman, like De Haan but not De Haan, Vincent-somebody. Listen to this letter: 'Gauguin interests me very much as a man, very much. With Gauguin, blood and sex prevail over ambition.' Charming no?

GAUGUIN: Very much, Emile – he flatters me 'cause he's honest! Anymore, Mrs G?

GLOANEC: Monsieur Louis Anquetin...

GAUGUIN: Anquetin, painter of: 'Avenue de Clichy: Five O'Clock in the evening' - unusual angles, sharp perspectives, cropped figures, ideas lifted from Japanese prints.

(He taps the image)

He lent us a book: 'The Marriage of Loti' – a French man shaggin' his way round Tahiti – phwoargh! Now, fair enough, *maybe* I accidentally mixed it up with stories of me own of sailors abandoned on tropical islands full of naked tarts, which I suppose is *maybe* why me friend Charlie Laval and me (and thousands of other Frenchmen) ended up in Panama in a disastrous attempt to repeat the Suez success: by linking the Pacific with the Caribbean. It was only 60 kilometres – what's that in miles? - but five hundred thousand million francs and 20,000 dead from malaria? No thanks. We cleared out and went to Martinique, lived in an auld doss, ate what we could scavenge and painted the same views - hard to tell one from the other - but I began to feel a style evolving. We returned to Paris in '87, sick as dogs but knowing we'd experienced something that'd affected our work. Unfortunately the Parisian critics didn't share our enthusiasm and poor Charlie snuffed it in Egypt soon after. And still I starved. But I produced work for the right to starve!

Science was making progress but the development of aestheticism was slow by comparison - you only had to glance at that bag of shite by Gustave Eiffel in Paris to realise that. Anthropologists had gone to the colonies and taken measurements of bones and catalogued pagan rituals and whatnot but none had gone to record the beauty of a disappearing Eden. So I went back to Brittany and me second new Dutch friend Vincent went to Arles. Brittany wasn't Tahiti, but better than Paris.

And then, suddenly – bosh! - I done it.

(He indicates: 'Jacob wrestling with the angel' or 'The Vision After the Sermon')

Tension 'tween the abstract and the natural, the real and the mystical. I *knew* summat had happened, felt it: a spirit passed into me body, manifested itself through that painting and then left again, moved on to enlighten another. I sacrificed everything – execution, colour, subject all for style. I used colour to express emotion instead of a reflection of the reality I saw. I've Emile Bernard to thank, in part – his 'Breton Shepherdesses' inspired it. And with it came a realization about myself, inspired by the subject matter: I wasn't the shepherd and I certainly wasn't the sheep, so what was I?

And Vincent and Arles? A marriage of convenience - Theo, his brother, offered to support us both with a little money if we kept on producing: me in Brittany, Vincent in Provence, but ultimately cheaper to have wuh both under the same roof and Provence won. Anyway, Theo had sold some of me work so I felt obliged.

He paid the rent and there was enough left over to buy important things like tobacco, absinthe, wine. A yellow house! I hated the place. It pissed doon all the time. Vincent lived like a pig and couldn't cook. All he did was drink and whore. But then, so did I. But he really *believed* in a Brotherhood of Art. In his 'brotherhood' I was to be the new 'Messiah', the head of his group. I took the piss summat chronic and threatened to leave but he gans nuts and it come to a head in a square in Arles - literally: he cuts off his ear! I know if I'd stayed he'd have had a go at us, so I legged it just before Christmas.

And in that vein, I seen an execution in Paris, January 1890, a murderer called Prado, Madame La Guillotine. The first attempt was botched - it sliced into his face. He lay there in agony drowning in his own blood, begging for death with half a tongue. And Death came, straddled the corpse like a triumphant warrior and cast its eyes round for its next victim – me. 'How did he die?' that's what they always ask. 'How did he live and how did he die?'

When I heard about Vincent's death, I was sad. Not surprised, but sad. After that I'd the feeling he was always there, a spirit, a shadow, haunting wuh, y'kna?

So I held an exhibition of work from Brittany and Martinique to raise funds and, funds raised, left for the South Seas early April, '91. Forty-third birthday, sighted Tahiti: *expected* half-naked buxom lasses to put flowers in me hair, lead us to a bower of palms and pina coladas and get their kits off. *Got* a gendarme whose white uniform was too big, harsh colonisation underway with the best land taken, expensive imported foodstuffs, Catholics, Protestants and native beggars with European diseases.

But it wasn't all bad: first there was Titi - a stupid lass who thought all European men had bottomless pockets but you divvent look at the mantelpiece when yer pokin' the fire - and then there was Teha'mana, canny Teha'mana with her pocketful of bottom. When not pre-occ'd with Teha'mana, I painted fast and furious – the colours, man, *the colours!* Yellow for the faces, red for the hair, blue for the clothes, purple for the mountains, a sleeping kitten for peace. When I couldn't afford canvas I used old boards, sackcloth, anything - thirty canvasses and carvings from that first trip. Set off back to France. Oor lass sat at the dockside and watched wuh go.

'Au revoir, Monsieur Paul! Je t'aime toujours !'

Oh aye, what's your name again? I couldn't think of nowt me 'cept I'd enough to shock the world. Back in Paris, started coughing blood.

'You've second stage syphilis, Monsieur Gauguin. You're also suffering from alcohol abuse. I'd estimate that you have perhaps ten years left, though it's hard to say and of course I'm not God.'

'Thanks for breaking it to us gently, Doctor,' I said.. But God was close wasn't he, finally conferring a blessing upon his disciple? Edgar!

DEGAS (RP): I've organised your first post-Tahiti exhibition, Gauguin - Paris. Don't hold your breath – the world isn't yet ready for you - but it's a start. Two of them: 'Hina Tefatou' and 'Te Faaturuma' - I'll take for myself. By the way, did you know your Uncle Isidore has died?

GAUGUIN: He was an auld tosser, Monsieur Degas. I hated him.

DEGAS: And left you 9,000 francs?

GAUGUIN: He was a great man, Monsieur Degas and will be sorely missed. Had up! Letter from the wife: 'My dear husband, please don't squander this inheritance. I ask nothing for myself but consider the children. You may be pleased to know that I'm slowly building up a collection of your work in Copenhagen and an increasing number of students and dealers want to see the pictures. If you don't succeed in Paris, you might always try Copenhagen.'

GAUGUIN: Copenhagen? Danish pastries! Why did I marry a woman from Copenhagen? Bollocks to that. I rented a studio in Rue Vercingetorix, Paris and had some *magnifique soirées:* Delius visited, as did Ravel, Greig, Debussy, a young German artist called Munch who complimented me on my wooden prints especially the swirling lines around the figures to emphasise movement, the Swedish writer Strindberg, the sculptor Rodin. With a wad of cash in me skyrocket and such illustrious company I was like a dog with two dicks when I met Anna the Javanese wandering lost in the Gare du Lyon. We went to Brittany again in '94, though I should've gone to Copenhagen. I give a good account of meself at Concarneau though in a scrap. You ever been kicked by wooden clogs? Made a gimp o' wuh, the bastards.

That did it for me - back to Tahiti. I took a lover: Pau'ura. Within months she was up the duff. I was over the Moon. But then one night I heard her voice under the Moon, beneath the stars: 'Mister Paul: the baby we make – she dead.'

Then a letter from Mette: 'My dear husband, it is with great difficulty and great sadness I must tell you that our daughter Aline has died. She was, as you know, only 19. It happened on New Year's Eve. She went to a Ball with friends. She looked so beautiful in her dress. She returned complaining of a chill and a week later she was gone.'

(He brings his face close to the small portrait of Aline on the collage)

My precious, precious Aline... they say an artist must suffer for his work but how much? How much must he suffer?

Up the spout again, Pau'ura finally gives us a bairn and the little Tahitian she taught wuh come in handy too: No te aha oe rir? Why are you angry? No te aha oe rir? Why are you angry? Why am I angry? Here was life beginning and I had life disintegrating!

So I leaves Tahiti and gans North, to the Marquesa Islands with some life left in wuh but knowing it was a one-way trip, to Hiva Oa and Father Martin who reminded us of Bishop Dupanloup.

MARTIN (French accent): Monsieur Gauguin, as you now know since arriving in Hiva Oa from Tahiti, all land hereabouts is owned by ze Church. To establish a home for yourself ze Church would need some evidence zat you concurred with its teachings, shall ve say? I've noticed since your arrival zat you've been present at morning Mass almost everyday. I know nozzing of your reputation as an artist but I'm impressed vizz your reputation as a believer. It will zerefore be our pleasure to sell you a piece of land upon which you may build a 'ome.

GAUGUIN: Aw hey, cheers marra! But guess what? As soon as the ink's dry I'll stop attending your stupid Mass, build me house and find a tasty young bit - Vaeoho. Oh hey, divvent gan forcing your twenty-first century, European, quasi-Christian values on us out here and divvent look at us like that, man: in Polynesia the art of love's as natural as your first walking steps. There's nae blokes on wooden crosses or shirts telling wuh it's

52

wrong or shirts an ties on telly saying: 'My client would like to deny that he has never had intimate relations with an under age girl.' Most of you's have never seen a jungle. The jungle doesn't give a fuck about that. The jungle consumes everything, man, everything: religion, morality, law, right, wrong, good, bad, all that's drilled into wuh from birth in the so-called civilized world, the jungle consumes - as will the earth consume me and you. An abundance of foliage and nature gone mad and we cannot help but replicate that abundance. Only when faced with the jungle did I realise just how primitive I was. Somebody should tell that to those in Europe. I reckon they've forgot. Those fucking European always want to force onto the rest of the world their own hypocritical morality. I didn't rape her, for God's sake1 I didn't force her! She came to my bed willingly! Her parents encouraged her! For them it was a sign of status that her daughter would carry a white man's child.

I built up a small collection of flowers: dahlias, nasturtiums. Me dealer told us flowers were popular but only French flowers of course. In France they said the native flowers in Polynesia were too fantastic to be true!

And Pastor Vernier befriended us - a Proddy! He kept us supplied with the morphine I needed to cope as the clap kicked in and me body fell to bits.

'I'm going to get your soul, Gauguin! I vill 'ave vengeance!' says Father Martin to us one day. 'But, if I take my own life, Father, me poor soul'll be tainted, dirty, unclean, unfit to enter the spotless kingdom of your God,' I says, though it wasn't the first time I'd thought of topping myself. 'I doubt you 'ave ze courage,

Gauguin, You're not ze Dutchman you talk about so much, what vas 'is name, Van Gogh?'

GAUGUIN: Vincent, Vincent?

VAN GOGH (Dutch accent): How are you, Paul, meinen old friend? Don't be afraid - you chose zis route to buy a few more years und look at what you've produced. I, on ze uzza 'and, got ze short straw. I could've done so much more. For ze incident in Arles I apologise, Paul. I vas angry you couldn't share meinen vision. You know, our influence will filter down through something as zimple as a drawing zat 'angs on a bedroom wall or a picture on a postcard. Now zat's revolution. Ze camera changed everything but you, you knew what had to be done: no longer could ze painter use ze canvas to reflect reality when ze camera did that much more effectively. We helped re-invent art and art – like God - brings hope. How do you want ze world to remember you? Show zem how you gave *everything* for what you believed in.

(He traces 'Self Portait at Golgotha')

'Self-Portrait, close to Golgotha' You see? It was always destiny. *You* must end it. Und, ven you've ended it, you und I vill zit in ze cafes of Paris like shadows, sip absinthe forever und watch ze beautiful girls.

GAUGUIN: Sounds canny, I'll just get me coat. Just a tick: Last Will and Testament of Eugene Henri Paul Gauguin: a dozen carvings, two easels, two palettes, record of military service, cotton trousers and shirts, mosquito net, tobacco and cigarette papers, tinned imported meats, a compass, some wood-working tools, a magnifying glass, a wrench, a green beret, a few bottles of absinthe, ten paintings and a cuddly toy - me life. Not much is it? All I've got left is me thoughts and here they are, for what they're worth: the world makes its true artists struggle and then takes their art from them and, with its education, its universities and its money, it pontificates on 'the nature of genius' or says the artist must suffer on the cross like a reluctant Jesus for the sins of the same world that put the artist there in the first place! And what are they? Avarice, envy, fear and stupidity, wrapped up as 'benevolence', 'courage' 'generosity' and 'love'.

Each day of my life's a war between the positive and the negative, the strong and the weak. The strong're not so easy to spot: they wear the same clothes at work as they wear at home and speak their minds and make no effort to be everybody's friend and if they tell the truth we still don't believe them because we don't want the truth. But beware the weak. You can spot them easy: they wear suits at work and designer gear at home and tell you, you cannot do what they cannot do, for the weak are more concerned with what others think of them than what they think of themselves.

I spent me last few hours listening to me auld friend and neighbour, the cannibal witch doctor Tioka, chanting his mumbo-jumbo about selling me immortality in return for surrendering me soul. He dictated his terms – it wasn't a bad deal and I signed on the dotted. So then I filled me syringe with a too-large dose of morphine and wrote one final letter to an old friend in Paris: 'Hiva Oa, April, 1903, to my old friend Charles Morice: Yes, I'm down but not yet defeated. In my opinion, artists have lost all their savagery, all their instinct; one might say their imagination. As a result they act only as undisciplined crowds and feel frightened, lost as it were, when they're alone. Solitude isn't to be recommended to everyone, for you have to be strong in order to bear it and act alone. Thus, I can say: no one taught me anything. On the other hand it's true I know so little, but I prefer that little that's my own creation and, who knows whether that little, when put to use by others, won't become something big?'

Within a few hours I was dead. Within half a day I was six foot under, thanks to Father Martin, no post-mortem. He smashed everything he didn't like and sold the rest to pay me fine. At the auction some pleb holds me last work 'Breton Snowscape' upside down and sold it as 'Niagra Falls'. Oh aye they all had a good laugh at that. But all these years later, who remembers their names? You want to live forever - you got to deliver the goods.

(End)

Tommy Greaves

When I first saw the film 'Billy Elliot' I thought: 'This is my story', but then I suppose many people who see that film think the same. But what always bugged me was that when I was a young man performing live poetry at various charity gigs around the North East in aid of striking miners, the writer of 'Billy Eliot' - Lee Hall - was, presumably, studying English at Cambridge University, a far contrast from the world he recreates in his film, a film at times funny and inspiring but also 'saccharin', I guess to keep the producers happy. So though I very much enjoy some of the sentiments in the film, I've always been unhappy about how Hall hadn't really penetrated some of the deeper divisions during that period. Perhaps he had but they ended up on the cutting room floor, I don't know.

At the age of 20 and 21, I was an 'angry young man' with limited education but a great passion for poetry, performance and playwriting. It was through acting that I finally became good enough to get a place at Central School of Speech and Drama in London in 1985. Though I chose acting and not dancing as my passport to liberation, what Hall barely touched on as Billy was still at school, Tommy Greaves/I endured.

I came up against a lot of resistance writing this, defending myself against accusations of plagiarism. But my best defence is to hold up a copy of my book 'Maggie Thatcher (my part in her downfall)' (my diaries from 1982 – 1985). Within those pages is an honest account of the self-awareness of a young man in North East England, so it's not like I'm making it up. Furthermore, the idea of the 'community centre' or

Church Hall was (and still is) strong in almost all villages and towns across the country and all kids got involved in various activities at some time or another. The Community Centre is the hub for many people but 'Billy Elliot' the script doesn't have the monopoly on activities there – in my day it was Darlington Drama Centre and Darlington Arts Centre. As for the sexual themes present in the film and in my script, growth and self-awareness through sexuality are universal and eternal key factors but at that time macho, working class society frowned on anything that wasn't heterosexual. The working class was strong but it was also reluctant to accept its limitations and inability to change, which is why I introduced the contrast of the entrepreneurial Tory-voter as Tommy's step-dad and in this was also able to exploit some of the themes in Hamlet. Either way, whether I write this or don't write it, I'm damned if I do and damned if I don't. I acknowledge the debt to Lee Hall for his film. I've never denied the connection. I think he does a good job highlighting some of the battles people faced in those days. I just wanted to go further and I see no shame in adapting from what I remember because I lived through it. The parallels between the film and my play are strong and I'm not denying it, but they're not competitive and, I hope, are taken as complementary. When I wrote to Lee Hall's agent with these ideas and then to Working Title, they came down on me like a ton of bricks and threatened me with all sorts of legal actions if I even so much as tried to connect my script with the film 'Billy Elliot', but nobody is taking my story away from me. The audience can decide. Anyway, I don't like bullies.

What was decided politically in those days laid the foundations for the myth of the so-called 'global village' of today. It is imperative we see the truth of this myth so that people can understand why the Miner's Strike, amongst other conflicts at that time, was so important and is so relevant. Any village has expensive houses and cheap houses, wealthy, educated citizens and poorer, less educated ones. Apply this logic to the world we live in today and we understand better how it is that a pair or Reeboks can be made in China for a few dollars but sold at ten times their value in London.

'Tommy Greaves' received a public reading in English in Paris on 16th November 2014. The organiser was Moving Parts hosted by Stefanie Campion at Carr's Bar. The readers were: Damian Corcoran, Roger Surridge, Maja Bieler, Mollie Keane, Mona Morgen and Peter Vickers and Johnny Palmer. I am deeply indebted to the actors and Stefanie for the insight their work gave me.

Cast:

TOMMY GREAVES, 15
GEORGE (FRIEND OF TOMMY'S LATE FATHER), 40's
GORDON (TOMMY'S STEPFATHER), 30's
BRENDA GREAVES (TOMMY'S MOTHER), 30's
MR WALLACE (TOMMY'S HEAD TEACHER), 50's
GHOST OF DAD (TOMMY'S LATE FATHER), 40's
JULIE LOWES, (TOMMY'S GIRLFRIEND), 15
BARRY PROSSER (DRAMA TEACHER), 40's
DETECTIVE PALMER (POLICE), 40's
ALAN (TOMMY'S YOUNGER FRIEND), 13
MR LOWES (JULIE'S DAD), 50's
RADIO NEWSREADER, VOICE OVER and CROWD VOICES

Tommy Greaves

Act One

1.

(Street Market. TOMMY GREAVES, 15, unzips his hold-all and brings out a porno magazine FIESTA, one vinyl LP 'Welcome to the Pleasure Dome' album, video cassettes 'Quest For Fire', 'Mad Max 2', two RELAX t-shirts on coat hangers, Adidas trainers and Doc Marten boots in the boxes and brand new tools – a Black & Decker claw hammer and a saw still with wrappers. Keeping a cautious eye in all directions, TOMMY has become a salesman of stolen goods.)

TOMMY. Rights lads and lasses, fresh off the back of a lorry, fresh off the backs of various lorries! Ask no questions and I'll tell you no lies! (He brandishes the porn magazines) Everything you need to now about sex education but were afraid to ask! (He brandishes the pop album) Top 40 LP's with the latest hits! (He brandishes the videos) Brand new videocassettes: Raiders of the Lost Ark and Star Wars! (He brandishes one 'Frankie Says Relax' t-shirt) Top quality in small, small and small again!

(A group of men chanting: 'Coal - not - Dole!' nearby competes with TOMMY'S pitch. He tries to shout above them)

TOMMY. Straight out of the factory – tools to make every handyman happy! (In the direction of the shouting men) Oy! Give it a rest will you? Some of us are trying to make some money here!

(Enter GEORGE, 40's, a protesting miner carrying a COAL NOT DOLE placard, an old friend of TOMMY'S late Dad)

GEORGE. Why aren't you at school, Tommy?

TOMMY. Got the day off.

GEORGE. Where'd you get all this gear?

TOMMY. Jumble sale. Using me noggin to make some extra brass, George.

GEORGE. You're a fly bugger and no mistake. Listen, best make yourself scarce, kid – we're expecting the police soon and then it'll kick off. Go on, away with you. I'll see you down the Social Centre later.

(Exit GEORGE to rejoin the protesting miners. TOMMY pretends to pack away his gear but as soon as GEORGE has gone, starts selling again.)

TOMMY. Ladies and gents its bargain time in Boomtown – make me an offer I can't refuse!

(Sound of a police siren)

TOMMY. Fuck!

(TOMMY hastily repacks his holdall, not in fear of the police but because of the inconvenience. Cue: 'Love of the Common People' by Paul Young 'Living in the love of the common people, smiles from the heart of the family man, papa's gonna buy you a dream to cling to, mama's gonna love you just as much as she can, and she can'.)

2.

(TOMMY, 15, and his Mam BRENDA'S new boyfriend GORDON, 30's, eat breakfast. GORDON wears a long blue apron, a white cap and has a pencil tucked behind his ear. TOMMY is dressed ready for school. BRENDA, in dressing gown, pours tea.)

RADIO NEWSREADER VOICE-OVER: 'Arthur Scargill, President of the National Union of Mineworkers, has today ruled out a national ballot of miners on whether to continue their strike, which has already lasted five weeks. Meanwhile official figures today confirmed that more than 100 pickets were arrested in violent clashes in Derbyshire and Nottinghamshire three days ago. Sad news though, the great comedian Tommy Cooper sadly died of a heart attack last night while filming 'Live From Her Majesty's'. He was 62.'

(GORDON turns off the radio)

GORDON. Just like that! Do you get it? Tommy Cooper died - just like that? Tommy Cooper? That was his catchphrase.

(No response from TOMMY or BRENDA)

BRENDA. This bloody strike: pig-headed men versus more pig-headed men. It's tearing this town apart – everybody'll be up at the picket line today.

GORDON. Not everybody Brenda, the world doesn't turn around miners. Anyway, while they're kicking each other's heads in, their wives'll be down the market haggling for cheap fish to put on the table when they get home and I'll be there to take their money off them. I might be late back tonight - I'm driving out to Tynemouth to see what the trawler men have brought in. They won't be going on strike, thank buggery. By the way, Tommy, I tried to see you on your market stall last week but couldn't find you. I didn't know which stall you were on.

TOMMY (evasive). Depends – the bloke I work for moves around a lot.

GORDON. Well he must be pleased with you, you're never short of a few bob. I could use a good worker for our stall but it wouldn't be right if I got a pitch in the market and you were working for another outfit.

TOMMY (evasive). No it wouldn't.

BRENDA. I have to go Tommy's school this morning to see the Head of Year.

GORDON. Oh aye? Everything all right at school is it?

TOMMY. Why don't you mind your own business?

BRENDA. Tommy, don't start.

GORDON. It's all right, Brenda. It is my business.

TOMMY. It's nowt to do with you me life.

GORDON. Your Mam and me want to see you do well in the world, son.

TOMMY. I'm not your son.

GORDON. It's just a figure of speech, look I may not know much, according to you, but I do know the days of apprenticeship are on the way out and the age of entrepreneurs is just round the corner and a decent bit of education will give you that edge.

TOMMY (to BRENDA). Dad's only been gone six months and a fishmonger's took his place, living here, sleeping in your bed, sitting at our table, stinking the place out!

BRENDA. Don't talk like that about Gordon. Gordon's hard-working.

TOMMY. So was Dad.

BRENDA. He wasn't Snow White, Tommy.

TOMMY. He worked hard. He put food on the table.

BRENDA. And shall I spend forever in mourning sitting around depressed with the curtains closed?

TOMMY. It's only six months. And Gordon's a Tory - I can't believe you've let a Tory sit at our table.

BRENDA. What do you know about all that, Tommy? You're only 15, still at school.

TOMMY. Dad would have been out there today on the Picket Line with the other miners fighting for his job!

BRENDA. Aye and we'd be sitting here in the cold. There'd be no breakfast, no central heating and you'd be wearing cast-off's. Gordon gave me a job on the fish stall, a job Tommy. Do you know how precious they are round here? No you don't coz you're only 15 and know nothing about the world. With your Dad I was stuck in all day long. 'A woman's place is in the home!' he used to say like somebody out of Charles Dickens.

GORDON. It's every man for his self in this world, Tommy.

TOMMY (to GORDON). I know all about fighting, Mr Fishmonger. (to MAM) What's happened to you in only a few months?

BRENDA. I loved your Dad, Tommy, I always will, but don't romanticise the past like butter wouldn't melt in his mouth. Gordon's like your Dad was once when we were younger.

TOMMY. He's nothing like me Dad. You're nothing like me Dad.

GORDON. Your Dad's a hard act to follow, Tommy. He saw things a certain way and I see things differently. I didn't want to go down the pit when I was your age. It's a horrible life – claustrophobic, dangerous, dirty.

Anyway, there's no future down the pit - there never was, not for me, but now there's no future for anybody.

TOMMY. The miner's are striking for better wages.

GORDON. But they're not though, Tommy – they're striking cause Arthur Scargill told them to strike. About them all losing their jobs, he's totally right, about winning the strike he's totally wrong.

(BRENDA makes signs to GORDON to change the subject)

GORDON. Look, your exams'll be coming up soon, O Levels and that. Listen, I'll give you £20 every exam you pass, how does that sound? That's an incentive.

TOMMY. I don't want your money. I don't want nowt from you.

(GORDON shrugs at BRENDA. Cue: 'Tears of a Clown' by The Beat 'Now if there's a smile on my face, it's just there trying to fool the public, but when it comes down to losing you, now honey that's quite a different subject, don't let my sad expression give you the wrong impression'.)

3.

(TOMMY'S School. TOMMY and BRENDA seated side-by-side waiting for the arrival of the Head of Year, MR WALLACE.)

TOMMY. Grandad went the same way – heart attack.

BRENDA. The smoking, drinking and working underground didn't do him any favours.

TOMMY. The same is going to happen to me. It runs in the family.

BRENDA. Don't be daft. You're only 15, Tommy – you've got years ahead of you. (Impatient to be elsewhere) Look, did the Head give you any idea at all what this is about? I should be at the shop.

TOMMY. If I'm going to die of a heart attack twenty years from now, what's the point in doing anything?

BRENDA. Stop it, Tommy. You're not going to die twenty years from now.

TOMMY. Thirty! Forty! What difference does it make? What's the point? What's the point in exams, work, school, if we're all going to end up like Dad?

(Enter MR WALLACE, 50's, Headmaster, files under his arm, half-moon glasses on the bridge of his nose)

WALLACE. Apologies for the lateness, Mrs Greaves – we've had our work cut out because of the strike - a few playground scuffles between striking miners kids and non-striking miners kids – class war behind the bike sheds. 'The Ragged Trousered Philanthropists' might be highly instructional to our youth at this time.

BRENDA. Pardon?

WALLACE (aware he's talking beyond her capacity for understanding). Forgive me. Could you wait outside please, Tommy? I think it's best I speak to your mother alone.

(WALLACE and BRENDA sit apart. TOMMY strains to listen.)

WALLACE. Has Tommy explained why I've asked you in?

BRENDA. No.

WALLACE. I see. Well, to put it bluntly, you do know last week we had the exams?

BRENDA. Last week? But I'm sure Tommy told me it was next week?

WALLACE. It was last week.

BRENDA. Oh, right. I – I don't quite –

WALLACE. Tommy was absent from all of them, Mrs Greaves.

BRENDA. Absent? What – what do you mean, 'absent'?

WALLACE. I mean: 'not present'. All of last week the entire fifth year of the school sat their examinations - GCSE's or CSE's - and Tommy was absent from every single one of them.

BRENDA. But – but he told me the exams were - what does that - ?

WALLACE. It means, in no uncertain terms, Tommy will be leaving the school very shortly with absolutely no qualifications whatsoever.

(TOMMY exits)

BRENDA. What, none at all?

WALLACE. His name was on the list for three O Levels and four CSE's but he failed to appear.

BRENDA. But – but I thought – what, *none* of them?

WALLACE. You weren't aware of anything being amiss? Forgive me, would you like my secretary to bring you a cup of tea?

BRENDA. No. No thank you.

WALLACE. If it's any consolation, he can be disruptive at times and argumentative but there's no doubting his intelligence, unfortunately he seems to hold himself in low regard. His schoolwork is adequate – not exceptional, you understand, but adequate.

I understand your late husband passed away last year? That must have been, well, perhaps traumatic is an understatement. That kind of event can have adverse effects on one's emotional balance and mood swings.

BRENDA. Can't he sit them again?

WALLACE. Not just now, though special dispensation might be arrived at later in the year. Look, perhaps we

70

can get him in to try and find out what's going in? Tommy, can you come in please! Tommy? Tommy?

(Cue: 'One in Ten' by UB40 'I am a one in ten, a number on a list, I am a one in ten, even though I don't exist. Nobody knows me but I'm always there, statistical reminder of a world that doesn't care'.)

4.

(At The Community Centre. TOMMY and GEORGE are both eating)

GEORGE. There's one hot meal a day here at the canteen for strikers. The wife's a clever cook – she made this what we're eating now.

TOMMY. Did she? It's well tasty, George.

GEORGE. I only come down here to the Centre for the crack and to be with the lads, not much else to do when you're on strike.

TOMMY. How was it today on the picket?

GEORGE. Brutal - they're bringing in coppers from other parts of the country.

TOMMY. Are you going to win?

GEORGE. They've got us on the ropes Tommy if ever a boxing ring was a metaphor for the world outside the boxing ring, which it is I suppose.

TOMMY. I should be there. Dad would have been.

GEORGE. Don't be daft. Stay away, Tommy.

TOMMY. So why bother?

GEORGE. What else am I supposed to do? They're me mates – you always stick by your mates. But Scargill's a dipstick for starting the strike in March.

TOMMY. Why?

GEORGE. Spring's here.

TOMMY. So?

GEORGE. So Summer's next and then Autumn and who needs coal fires at these times? It'll be next Winter before things get rough: that's nine long months of jumble sales, baked beans and hand-me-downs. Still, we survived Hitler, I'm sure we can survive Thatcher. How about your Mam? How are you coping since you lost your Dad?

TOMMY. I wouldn't mind me Dad being dead so much if it wasn't for me Mam living with somebody else in such a short time. It's not right.

GEORGE. Funny things are women, funny things. You see her as a mother and I see her as a friend – somewhere between those two things you've got to try and understand her. I still can't believe your Dad's gone sometimes it was so sudden – a sobering reminder to live for today. But hey, you'll be leaving school soon.

TOMMY. I already have.

GEORGE. Will you be going for an apprenticeship?

TOMMY. I don't know what I'll be going up for.

GEORGE. Back in my days you'd leave school Friday afternoon and be in a job on Monday morning. Apprenticeships were what it was all about – a trade. What about hobbies - things to do when there's nowt else? And let's face it: there *is* nowt else round these parts but hobbies can lead to trades.

TOMMY. What hobbies?

GEORGE. There's boxing – though kicking heads in was never much of a trade unless you joined the police force. What about judo?

TOMMY. What, like Kung Fu? I'm no Bruce Lee.

GEORGE. There's painting. With brushes and proper canvases and that, like Van Gogh.

TOMMY. Watching paint dry? No thanks.

GEORGE. There's stamp collecting.

TOMMY. That's for anoraks.

GEORGE. There's flower arranging – no, stupid of me. What about drama? Some actor bloke, he does these acting classes once a week.

TOMMY. What, like acting like in the films and that?

GEORGE. Aye. They say he's been on telly a few times but I've never heard of him.

TOMMY. Being on telly sounds all right.

GEORGE. Thursday nights. 50 pee. Better than hanging 'round street corners eh?

TOMMY. Aye maybe. Oh I don't know George, I want to do something different with me life but I don't know what. Does everybody go through this stage – doing a lot of daft dreaming before they settle down just like everybody else?

GEORGE. Time spent dreaming is only wasted if you're getting paid to do something else but on its own time spent dreaming is precious, Tommy. You'll work it out. Here I tell you what, I love me wife's dumplings!

(The innuendo sinks in and they laugh. Cue: 'I Just Called To Say I Love You' by Stevie Wonder.)

5.

(TOMMY and JULIE snogging. JULIE has a small transistor radio. They listen to the pop music of the end of the previous scene. TOMMY pulls away.)

JULIE. What's the matter?

TOMMY. I fucking hate Radio 1. They won't play 'Relax' coz they say it's mucky. Who the fuck are Mike

Read and DLT and Noel Edmonds and Simon Bates and all them old BBC tossers to preach to us anyway?

JULIE. All right, keep your hair on.

(JULIE turns off the radio)

JULIE. They so some good telly programmes – Not The Nine O'Clock News and The Young Ones, so they can't all be bastards.

TOMMY. Here, what's that drama class about down at the Centre?

JULIE. Plays and acting, Shakespeare and that.

TOMMY. William Shakespeare? I've heard of him. We read one of his plays at school.

JULIE. Which one?

TOMMY. Hamlet.

JULIE. We did 'Romeo and Juliet', 'Romeo, Romeo, wherefore art thou, Romeo?'

TOMMY. 'To be or not to be that is the question' that's what we did. It was fucking mental. The teacher tried to explain it all but I couldn't make head or tail of it.

JULIE. Tommy, do you want to have sex with us?

TOMMY. Did Juliet say that to Romeo?

JULIE. I'm saying it to you. We've been going out for ages now Tommy and all we ever do is kiss and cuddle. What about the real thing? Are you scared? It's all right - I know what to do.

TOMMY. How do you know what to do like?

JULIE. I just do.

TOMMY. Are you on the Jack and Jill?

JULIE. Not yet. Me Mam won't let us. You could use a johnny. Have you got any johnnies?

TOMMY. Aye, I nicked some from Boots. Not used them yet like but I had a wank wearing one to see what it was like.

JULIE. You had a wank wearing a Johnny?

TOMMY. Aye, just to see what it was like.

(She laughs)

TOMMY. Don't laugh! It's like having a balloon on the end of me knob!

(She laughs more)

TOMMY: And there's that new disease everybody's talking about now as well, the one for homos. If it's not thing, it's another.

JULIE. You can pull your cock out at the last minute I suppose?

TOMMY. Yuk! Messy though shooting it all over your belly!

JULIE. I think it might be safe if you do it inside me when I'm on but that'll be pretty messy as well.

TOMMY. Oh Jesus aye, fucking gross - blood and spunk! Yuk fucking yuk! If we do it when you've got your period, can you not get pregnant like?

JULIE. I'm not sure, that's the only problem with Catholic school: nobody's sure of nowt, soon as the subject comes up everybody starts coughing. One thing I do know is if I do get pregnant, I get a council flat.

TOMMY. I don't want a baby or a council flat.

JULIE. But you want to leave home though don't you?

TOMMY. Fucking right.

JULIE. Well then?

TOMMY. But there has to be easier ways.

JULIE. Having babies is a serious business.

TOMMY. Being an adult is a serious business.

JULIE. Is it true you fucked your exams?

TOMMY. Aye.

JULIE. That's mad that! That's not serious at all. How are you going to get a job?

TOMMY. I don't want a fucking job! Everybody keeps going on at me like the future is so fucking inevitable – it's the Army, apprentice welder or down the pit – none of them need any of the crap they tried to teach me at school apart from fucking Metal Work and I hated that. What do I need exams for? My Dad didn't get any exams.

JULIE. I'm going to be a SEN nurse me.

TOMMY. What's an SEN?

JULIE. State Enrolled Nurse. Work for the NHS. Job for life is the NHS.

TOMMY. A nurse? How the fuck are you going to do that like?

JULIE. Got an appointment with the Careers Officer next week. She's going to help me.

TOMMY. Well you can't be a nurse and have a baby at the same time, can you?

JULIE. I don't see why not – a working Mother. All I'd need a bloke for is the baby. I could support meself.

TOMMY. This bloke me Mam's got living with us says different things to what me Dad said and he's a Tory. I'm ashamed to live there! How can he not see that Thatcher and all her cronies is the mortal enemy of the working class? It's like I've got a traitor living under the same roof. Me Dad would have battered him.

JULIE. Your Dad would have battered anybody.

TOMMY. Aye that was the only problem.

JULIE. What are you going to do, Tommy, to find a job? You're too young for dole.

TOMMY. Fuck knows but I'm not going down the pit and I'm not going to be a fucking welder. Here, is it true your Mam's run off with another bloke?

JULIE. Aye, he's got his own house in Sunderland. She reckons they'll be plenty of new jobs in the car factory the Japs are going to build. She wants me to go and live with her but then Dad'll be alone and have nobody to cook for him. He can't even boil an egg.

TOMMY. Aye and you'd be living among fucking Mackems. What a fucked-up world, isn't it Julie? It's nothing like they said it was going to be.

JULIE: Fancy another snog?

TOMMY. Aye all right but no shagging. You can put your hand down me pants and give us a wank instead.

JULIE: Oh I love romantic men.

(They snog. Cue: 'The Lunatics Have Taken Over the Asylum' by Funboy Three. 'Go nuclear the cowboy told us, and who am I to disagree, but when the madman flicks the switch, the nuclear will come for me'.)

6.

(Darkness. TOMMY is in bed dreaming, restless. GHOST OF DAD, in string vest, Jeannes and boots appears at the end of his bed. TOMMY sits up.)

TOMMY. Dad? Is that you?

GHOST OF DAD. Aye, I'm a ghost now – the Ghost of Dad.

TOMMY. What's it like, being a ghost?

GHOST OF DAD. Rubbish.

TOMMY. What's heaven like?

GHOST OF DAD. There is no Heaven.

TOMMY. So are you in Hell then?

GHOST OF DAD. There's no Hell either.

TOMMY. So where are you then?

GHOST OF DAD. Everywhere. Just not solid.

TOMMY. What's it like?

GHOST OF DAD. Dead boring – I can go to pubs, bars and betting shops but I can't drink beer or put money in fag machines or play the bandits or nowt.

TOMMY. Do you good. Hey, the miners are on strike, just like you said they'd be.

GHOST OF DAD. Aye I heard.

TOMMY. And Mam's got a new bloke living in the house.

GHOST OF DAD. She didn't waste much time did she?

TOMMY. That's what I said but that's not the worst of it.

GHOST OF DAD. Can it be worse?

TOMMY. He's a Tory.

GHOST OF DAD. Is he? Well, everybody has to be something, don't they? I mean if he wasn't a Tory then we'd have no need of Socialists.

TOMMY. Are you not bothered?

GHOST OF DAD. There's other things to worry about when you're dead, Tommy. It's you I'm worried about.

TOMMY. You needn't worry about me, Dad. I'll be all right.

GHOST OF DAD. You buggered your exams, you silly sod. What you do that for?

TOMMY. I don't need exams if I'm going to end up down the pit or in a factory.

GHOST OF DAD. But that's just the point, kid: there ain't gonna be no pits and no frigging factories neither and there's this new thing coming along called the microchip - a little thing that goes in computers, like in Star Trek. It's going to change everything and things are going to get worse before they'll get better.

TOMMY. Why did you used to get drunk and beat Mam up?

GHOST OF DAD. Oh Tommy, don't go on about that please. I can't change what I've done. I wish I could but I can't. Just try to learn from my mistakes is all I ask. Anyway, I've been sober a while now – well, no choice when you're dead. Oh and by the way, the serpent that did sting thy father's life now wears his crown.

TOMMY. Pardon?

GHOST OF DAD. The serpent that did sting thy father's life, now wears his crown.

TOMMY. I've heard that before somewhere.

GHOST OF DAD. It's from Hamlet, you dozy bugger. I'm trying to be cryptic.

TOMMY. Serpent? What, you mean like – like a snake? You mean – you mean Gordon killed you?

GHOST OF DAD. No, it was tabs, beer and too much lard that killed us. But he took me life, me wife, me bed and *now* he's trying to take me son.

TOMMY. No fear of that Dad. He'll never get me.

GHOST OF DAD. Glad to hear it. But I see you're getting in deeper with your thieving, Tommy - I'm disappointed. You'll come to a bad end with that mark my words. You get nothing for nothing in the world. If everything grew on trees we'd have no need for ambition and you need a little to get some learning done.

TOMMY. I'll jack it in soon, Dad, promise.

GHOST OF DAD. Don't lie to me, Tommy or I'll clatter you! I know you're lying. Actions count in the world, not talk so put your money where your mouth is, otherwise keep it shut. Well, sun's up shortly. I'd best be on me way or I'll turn into a pumpkin. Now get yourself down that Community Centre or Job Centre and get sorted with summat useful, do you hear me?

TOMMY. Yes, Dad.

GHOST OFDAD. Good. Now go back to sleep.

(TOMMY lies back down. Cue: 'Mad World' by Tears for Fears 'I find it kind of funny, I find it kind of sad, the dreams in which I'm dying are the best I've ever had, I find it kind of fearful because I find it hard to take, when people run in circles it's a very, very mad world'.)

7.

(The Community Centre. BARRY PROSSER, 50's, and TOMMY. BARRY is struggling trying to find the end of a roll of tape to tear off a strip to pin a flyer to the wall.)

TOMMY. Wanna hand?

BARRY. I haven't got fingernails.

TOMMY. I have. Let me try.

(TOMMY takes the roll and finds it easily and hands it back to BARRY)

BARRY. Long fingers, clean nails – the sign of an artist.

TOMMY. Are you the drama bloke?

PROSSER. I am the gentleman responsible for running the weekly drama club, yes. This is the flyer.

(TOMMY studies the flyer)

TOMMY. Acting and that, like on the telly?

PROSSER. And your name is?

TOMMY. Tommy. Tommy Greaves.

PROSSER. Barry Prosser.

(He reaches out his hand but TOMMY stares blankly. It's not a habit TOMMY is familiar with.)

PROSSER. I could say I teach acting but more often than not such skills are gifts people have, often without knowing it and certainly not knowing how to harness them. Perhaps it's safer to say I'm a guide rather than a teacher. Do you have any experience?

TOMMY. There's nowt like that at me school.

PROSSER. Do you have experience of amateur dramatics?

TOMMY. I don't have any experience at all.

PROSSER. Do you know anything about theatre?

TOMMY. I went to see Aladdin once and Shakespeare's theatre isn't it?

PROSSER. Ah, so you're familiar with the words of The Bard?

TOMMY. The what?

PROSSER. The Bard.

TOMMY: What's that like?

PROSSER: The Bard is a title given to a teller of great stories, among which is counted the son of a mid-sixteenth century Warwickshire merchant.

TOMMY. What's that go to do with Shakespeare?

PROSSER (patient but polite). Are you familiar with Shakespeare?

TOMMY. I know a bit of Hamlet. We did it at school. Have you been on telly?

PROSSER. I have had that honour.

TOMMY. What did you do?

PROSSER. Theatre and adverts - I did a few adverts.

TOMMY. No films?

PROSSER. No, no films.

TOMMY. What sort of adverts?

PROSSER. Forgettable adverts that paid the bills as most adverts do.

TOMMY. What about theatre? Have you done any plays in a proper theatre?

PROSSER. Yes a few and a few Shakespeare plays.

TOMMY. In London?

PROSSER. And Leeds, Glasgow, Newcastle, Manchester and Workington.

TOMMY. Workington?

PROSSER. It's not all glory.

TOMMY. Are you famous?

PROSSER. Hardly.

TOMMY. Why not?

PROSSER. Part chance, part choice. I spent three years studying acting in London as a young man.

TOMMY. But if you spend three years studying it in London why aren't you famous?

PROSSER. Because I can't just take the money and shut my mouth – I want to speak out about things that matter. So I became a teacher. There's no united front in the arts – how we could change the world if there was, but there isn't. Instead, there's vanity, greed, arrogance, insecurity and stress and either far too much money or far too little and the world of art is funnelled through a narrow tunnel by out-of-touch, middle class, Establishment intellectuals. Apart from that everything's perfect.

TOMMY. Er, right. So can you teach me to be a film star?

PROSSER. That's not a question I can answer. I might be able to guide you but the outcome isn't in my hands or yours. Your audience decides. Why would you want to be an actor?

TOMMY. I want to be rich and drive big cars and live in a big house and have loads of birds chasing me down the street.

PROSSER. Ah, a fellow idealist. All right, Tommy, find a Shakespeare speech, learn the lines and come back to me next week and we'll see what we can do.

(He starts to leave)

TOMMY. We can start now. I've got 50p.

PROSSER. You know some Shakespeare?

TOMMY (reading without stress or punctuation). 'To be or not to be that is the question whether 'tis nobler in the mind to suffer the slings and arrows of outrageous fortune or to take arms against a sea of troubles and by opposing end them to die to sleep no more and by a sleep to say we end the heartache and the thousand natural shocks that flesh is heir to 'tis a consumption devoutly to be wished. To die, to sleep, to sleep perchance to dream'

PROSSER. Not bad.

TOMMY. I can remember the words easy enough but I can't say I know what I'm talking about. Can you learn us what they mean?

PROSSER. Well, to know *that* it helps to know something about the play.

TOMMY. Do you know something about the play?

PROSSER: Is the Pope Catholic?

(Cue: 'Everything Counts' by Depeche Mode 'The grabbing hands grab all they can, everything counts in large amounts')

8.

(Home. GORDON and BRENDA at the kitchen table looking anxious, listening to the previous music track.)

BRENDA. Since this exams business I've not seen head nor tail of him. He's out God knows where at all hours. I got angry with him and he just curled up in a ball, so I tried a softly, softly approach and he got bossy and told me to mind my own business. I don't know what to do, Gordon.

GORDON. I've been out looking for him but just coz I can't see or find him doesn't mean he can't see and avoid me.

NEWS READER VOICE-OVER: 'Clashes yesterday at Orgreave colliery between 5,000 police and a similar number of striking miners has left 51 picketers and 72 policemen injured. Leader of the NUM, Arthur Scargill, was today arrested and charged with obstruction.'

(The doorbell rings)

BRENDA. Tommy!

(GORDON goes out, answers. We heard muffled voices off. Enter DETECTIVE PALMER in plain clothes followed by GORDON.)

PALMER. Mrs Greaves?

(PALMER flashes his ID Card)

PALMER. Detective Sergeant Palmer. I'm investigating reports of stolen goods. I wonder is it possible to speak with your son Tommy?

BRENDA. He's not here.

PALMER. I see. Well, as you might know we're rather busy just now with the strike but it'd make life easier if you'd give me permission to look around his bedroom rather than go to the chew of getting a warrant. Would that be all right? I won't touch or take anything.

BRENDA. I don't see why not.

(PALMER exits into the house. GORDON turns off the radio. BRENDA starts to say something to GORDON but GORDON puts his finger to his lips. They stay this way for half a minute, neither speaking but torrents of thoughts reflected in their faces as they listen to the floorboards and stairs creaking. PALMER returns.)

PALMER. Nothing untoward as far as I can see: an average teenager's bedroom. Thanks for letting me look.

BRENDA. What's this about?

PALMER (to GORDON). Your Tommy –

GORDON. He's not mine. I'm just . . .

BRENDA. He's my son.

(PALMER sits down and pulls out a notebook he consults)

PALMER. You do realise your son was down the station for questioning over theft of private property last November?

BRENDA. November? But he never said anything to me.

PALMER. About the time you lost your husband I believe, Mrs Greaves? I read about it in the paper. I'm sorry. Perhaps he didn't want to upset you any further, your son?

GORDON. What's this about?

PALMER. Some chap up at the railway station had his fishing rod nicked out of the boot of his car. He made a Citizen's Arrest of Tommy and a couple of others - got them to the station, wanted them charged. We tried to bluff them into confessing but Tommy proved versatile and anyway without proof or witnesses we had to let them go. He's been seen recently down the market trying to pass off certain items that match the description of stolen goods.

BRENDA. What goods? Stolen from where?

PALMER. Odds and sods from shops mostly. There've been a few burglaries round town recently as the strike bites into family budgets but nothing out of the ordinary. There's no sign of anything in his bedroom and nothing in the garden shed – I took the liberty on my way up the garden path – and no finger prints yet neither but if anything more reliable comes up in the way of evidence your Tommy will be on our check-up list I think you should know that.

GORDON. What do you mean: 'he's been seen'? Who's seen him?

BRENDA. But he said he had a job on a market stall.

PALMER. He does – in a manner of speaking – his own: Tommy Greaves - Back of a Lorry Second Hand Goods Limited, unofficial.

BRENDA. You mean – you mean he's stealing?

PALMER. Somebody is.

BRENDA. But he told us he worked on a market stall.

PALMER. And you believe him?

BRENDA. Why would he lie? We can give him anything he wants.

PALMER. The Headmaster of Tommy's Secondary, Jack Wallace, and I went to school together. He mentioned Tommy's wasted his exams recently. Put his head in the lion's mouth – being a teenager is an expensive business and needs to be paid for by some means or other. Do you think the loss of his father has affected him in some way, Mrs Greaves?

BRENDA. I suppose.

PALMER. Your late husband was a character when he was alive, Mrs Greaves – many a night we found him under the town clock. I hope Tommy hasn't inherited any negative traits.

BRENDA. Since this business with his exams he's hardly been home. I don't know where he is these days. I'm at my wit's end.

GORDON. I can have a word with him.

PALMER. Do you have any influence?

GORDON. I don't know. I try. I mean, I'm not – I try.

PALMER. You're not a miner then Mr Jones?

GORDON. No – fishmonger. Self-employed. No fan of Scargill or the strike – fools to themselves as far as I can see. But I can only try to inspire him by example. How are you coping, with the strike?

PALMER. Just when we thought we were getting on top of things, building bridges and so forth, this comes along then the Home Secretary advises us to have a 'more vigorous interpretation' of our duties, whatever that means.

GORDON. What *does* it mean?

PALMER. There's a room down at the station and in that room is a table and a chair and a red telephone. Every night that telephone rings and a voice at the other end, we presume from somewhere down in London, dictates times, places and numbers of pickets like they're dishing out betting odds for a horse race. I never know from one day to the next where the lads will be sent. I just tell them to do their duty.

(He gets up to go)

PALMER. Have a word with Tommy. He's heading for a secure bunk in Borstal if he keeps it up. Get to him before we do.

(Cue: 'Two Tribes' by Frankie Goes To Hollywood 'When two tribes go to war, one is all that you can score')

9.

(Drama Class. TOMMY and PROSSER.)

PROSSER. Show us an action but don't speak. We have to guess what it is.

(TOMMY mimes putting on gloves, looking furtively around, quietly tiptoeing to a window, tracing a circle on the windowpane with fingers and thumb shaped into a crude diamond-cutting tool. He pulls out the 'pane' and reaches in and unlatches the window then climbs into the imaginary space and proceeds to quietly go through drawers looking for and pocketing valuables. For a moment he freezes, thinking he's heard a noise, but then continues, steals more and finally lets himself out.)

PROSSER. Burgling a house.

TOMMY. A garden shed actually.

PROSSER. You were convincing.

TOMMY: I'm not surprised.

PROSSER. But I think you'd make a better actor than you would a thief. At least it'd be legal.

TOMMY. It's just . . . acting: I feel like a bit daft, like a kid.

PROSSER. We're making things up, like kids. But a lot of actors think the audience is stupid and needs to be told they're watching something not real but we already know the situation's not real, that's why we're there.

What we want is to be convinced that we're seeing *is* real, or could be. You convinced me you were burgling a house or garden shed there, just for a fleeting moment.

TOMMY. What about Shakespeare?

PROSSER. What about him?

TOMMY. Are you going to teach me how to say it proper?

PROSSER. You want to recite a Shakespeare speech? It's a bit ambitious.

TOMMY. I want to act it.

PROSSER. Hamlet?

TOMMY. Aye Hamlet.

PROSSER. Do you know what it's about?

TOMMY. It's the most famous play in the world isn't it?

PROSSER. It helps if you understand motivation. It's one thing learning it as an English class subject but it's another thing acting it.

TOMMY. What do you mean?

PROSSER. Can you relate to Hamlet?

TOMMY. You tell me.

PROSSER. He sees the ghost of his dead father. The ghost tells him he was murdered and replaced by another man who then married his mother. The ghost demands revenge and Hamlet can do anything, absolutely anything, except take revenge on his dead father. He dumps his girlfriend. He calls his father a fishmonger. He thinks a lot about death. Can you relate to those?

TOMMY. Fuck yeah, more than a bit. But that's not the reason I want to do it.

PROSSER. What's the reason?

TOMMY. It makes he happy.

PROSSER. It makes you happy?

TOMMY. Yes – (mimicking the dour TV advert and the music) happiness is a cigar called Hamlet, the mild cigar from Benson and Hedges.

PROSSER. I think you'd make a better actor than you would a comedian as well. You've got potential, Tommy. You're fifteen –

TOMMY. Sixteen.

PROSSER. Sixteen, but crappy jokes aside, you've got the head of a man ten years older. That's what I call potential.

TOMMY (joking). My jokes aren't crappy you cheeky bastard!

(Cue: 'Ghost Town' 'This town is coming like a ghost town – why watch the youth fight against themselves? The government's leaving the youth on the shelves.' by The Specials)

10.

(GORDON and TOMMY. TOMMY carries on and puts down a heavy crate of fish. GORDON gives him £5.)

GORDON. How come you take this money but you won't take it other times?

TOMMY. Coz other times you're trying to buy me but when you ask me to do some lifting and carrying then I'll take your money because it's earned.

GORDON. So why won't you come and work with me?

TOMMY. Because you're a fucking fishmonger, Gordon - it's the most disgusting job on the planet.

GORDON. Money doesn't stink, Tommy, you just think about that when you're eating food on the table *my* hard work put there. I don't want to fight with you all the time, Tommy. I'm trying to make peace with you for your Mam's sake. You know, one thing your late Dad and me had in common, one thing we believed in?

TOMMY. What?

GORDON. Fighting – he chose the literal and with me it's fighting the urge to sit around on my arse all day thinking the world owes me a living.

TOMMY. That's what we're doing just now, up at the pithead, Gordon – fighting. The working class have to fight - not just the government and coppers but ourselves, fighting the urge not to give in and just say 'Yeah, fuck it, it's all about money so who gives a fuck about anyone else?' I'm working class and proud of it, Gordon. That's all I ever heard from my Dad since I was old enough to walk and talk. That's how it's always been. But what are you? A poor man who thinks voting Tory makes him clever.

GORDON. It's good to know who the enemy is but the government isn't the enemy, Tommy. Speaking of which, the police were round the house the other day.

TOMMY. What do you mean?

GORDON. Some detective. He had a look round your bedroom.

TOMMY. Did he have a warrant?

GORDON. No but he was persuasive and your Mam is very trusting. If its any consolation I wouldn't have let the nosey bastard in if it'd been my house but it's not my house.

TOMMY. A copper sniffing round my bedroom?

GORDON. Aye, freaky eh? But you must be enough ahead of the game to not leave anything incriminating lying about and I'll credit you with that piece of smartness. He said some chap had fishing rods stolen out of his car boot and you were suspected. Told me and your Mam the whole story about you getting taken to the station last year. You managed to keep that quiet from her.

TOMMY. I couldn't tell Mam about it, she was already upset about Dad.

GORDON: That's what I thought, but she felt very let down anyway. I'm not thinking about me Tommy, I'm thinking about your mother. I don't want to see her hurt. You think long and hard about what I've said, Tommy. You need to start making some choices because if you don't, other people are going to be making them for you and you might not always like the choices they make.

TOMMY. What's that supposed to mean?

GORDON. It means stop hanging around with losers, thinking you can get what you want by taking short cuts.

TOMMY. You should mind your own business, Gordon.

GORDON. Listen, smart-arse, we both know the market stall job is bollocks. You're up to no good. Fine - keep it up, you'll face the consequences but don't come running expecting us to bail you out. I don't give a shit you lied to me, it's no skin off my nose but it hurts your Mother and I won't stand for it, Tommy, I won't stand for it.

(GORDON picks up the three crates. ALAN, 13, arrives.)

GORDON. All right.

ALAN. All right. All right, Tommy.

TOMMY. All right, Alan.

GORDON. This one of your mates?

TOMMY. Aye, Alan – he's still at school.

GORDON. Stick in, son.

(GORDON exits)

ALAN. Is that your step Dad?

TOMMY. He's the bloke who thinks he can fit me Dad's shoes, but the only thing he'll be stepping into is his fucking grave if he doesn't watch his back.

ALAN. What's this about you going to drama club?

TOMMY. It's true.

ALAN. Do you go every week?

TOMMY. Aye.

ALAN. Are you any good?

TOMMY. The teacher says I am.

ALAN. Good - coz I nicked this from WH Smith's.

TOMMY. What is it?

(ALAN hands him a book)

ALAN: 'Shakespeare – Complete Works'

TOMMY. That's some fucking size, Alan.

ALAN. Well if you don't read it it'll come in useful for keeping doors open.

TOMMY. What else did you nick?

ALAN. Videos, Parker Pens and a couple of Commodore pocket calculators.

TOMMY. I'll see if I can't shift them, minus me usual commission.

ALAN. You should work for yourself you – you'd make a fortune.

TOMMY. I already do.

(TOMMY opens the book and turns some pages. They look together.)

ALAN. Who's that?

TOMMY (reading): Oliver, Laurence Oliver. Doing Hamlet.

ALAN. Why's he holding a skull?

TOMMY. He's contemplating death.

ALAN. That's not much of a job.

TOMMY. It is if you're a gravedigger. The skull belonged to a court jester called Yorick.

ALAN. Yorick? What was he like, a Paki?

TOMMY. It's a Danish name.

ALAN. What's he saying to it?

TOMMY. He's saying: 'Alas poor Yorick - he donated his body to science and only got a fiver.'

ALAN (serious). Did he?

TOMMY. Oh aye.

(PROSSER enters)

PROSSER (to ALAN). It's 50p to join in or free to leave.

ALAN. No fear. See you later, Tommy.

(ALAN exits)

PROSSER. Friend?

TOMMY. Alan his name is - everybody thinks he's a shirt-lifter, always getting picked on at school but live and let live's what I say. He knocks about with us coz I let him be.

PROSSER. That's a noble attitude and speaking of noble – what have you got for us, Prince Hamlet?

TOMMY. 'To be, or not to be, that is the question, Barry, whether 'tis nobler in the mind to suffer the slings and arrows of outrageous fortune, or to take arms against a sea of coppers and by opposing end them? To die, to sleep to sleep, perchance to win the strike!

PROSSER. No.

TOMMY. To die, to sleep no more, perchance to dream of winning the pools?

PROSSER. No.

TOMMY. To sleep, to die, to forget what comes next? I'm not giving up.

PROSSER. That's what I like to hear.

TOMMY. To die, to sleep, no more and by a sleep to say we end the heartaches and the thousand natural shocks that flesh is heir to, 'tis a consumption devoutly to be –

PROSSER. Consummation, not consumption!

TOMMY. I can't do this!

PROSSER. Look, this speech is one of the most - if not *the* most - famous speech in the world. Who doesn't know the opening line, if not the finishing line? How many thousands of actors have had to find some way to make these familiar words sound as if never heard before?

TOMMY. I don't know what half these words mean. It's about going on living or killing yourself, isn't it? To be

103

alive or not to be alive, right? A bare bodkin is a like a big needle – I looked it up in a dictionary – but what the fuck does 'quietus with a bare bodkin' fucking mean? It's fucking Chinese to me. 'This mortal coil' is life but what's a 'proud man's contumely'? And what's 'disprized love' and 'the law's delay'? 'Patient merit of the unworthy' 's got me bamboozled, what the fuck's that all about? Why didn't these old bastards speak proper English?

PROSSER. What's the book?

TOMMY (flicking through it): Shakespeare's Greatest Hits - present from Alan.

PROSSER. You're really taking this seriously.

TOMMY. Well, one of us is.

(Enter GEORGE, his donkey jacket ripped at the elbow, blood pouring down his face from a head wound.)

TOMMY. Fucking hell, George.

PROSSER. Come and sit down.

(GEORGE sits on a stool)

GEORGE. Coppers smashing heads! Coppers on horses!

(PROSSER takes paper towels to help staunch his head wound)

GEORGE. Standing minding me own and they laced in, belting us! Aye, she's on a roll after the Falklands!

104

PROSSER. She's a wicked old bitch - thinks if she can do it to the Argentines she can do it to her own.

GEORGE. Cameras were there – it'll be on the telly tonight. The world will see what she's doing.

PROSSER. This cut looks bad, George. You need to get to a hospital.

GEORGE. I'll walk it.

PROSSER. No, it's not safe – the police'll be picking on stragglers. I'll give you a lift. Tommy, we can cancel the class or you can work on your own.

(TOMMY and GEORGE exit)

TOMMY. To fight, or not to fight, that is the question . . .

(Cue: 'Vengeance' by New Model Army 'I believe in justice, I believe in vengeance, I believe in getting the bastard, getting the bastard, getting the bastard now'.)

11.

(BRENDA and TOMMY watch the Six O'clock News. GHOST OF DAD is also watching.)

TOMMY. Bastards.

GORDON. They attacked the police, throwing rocks and stones. You can see for yourself. That's your proud working class, Tommy – thugs, animals.

TOMMY. But that film looks like the pickets started it. That's not what I heard how it went.

GORDON. The camera never lies Tommy.

TOMMY. Aye the picture camera but surely with the film camera you can chop bits up and rearrange the running order! It's what Stalin and Hitler did – used film to manipulate what people think. George fucking Orwell – Nineteen Eighty-Four – we're there now and its all coming true and nobody gives a fuck!

GORDON. You're exaggerating a bit there aren't you, comparing the BBC to Hitler? However much you hate Maggie, don't suppose for one minute she's big enough to control the BBC.

TOMMY. Thatcher doesn't need to control anybody – it's fucking ingrained in middle class consciousness.

GORDON (sarcastic) Oh here we go, Karl Marx has joined us.

GHOST OF DAD. They're all in it together! All the other unions are helping the government, feeding them information about flying pickets and bus routes !

TOMMY (to GORDON). George from down the Centre said it was the coppers started it.

GORDON. Guilty men blame others, Tommy.

GHOST OF DAD. I wish I *was* too, too solid flesh again, kiddo, I'd take great pleasure flattenin' this twat.

BRENDA. It's giving me a headache the pair of you! Pack it in bickering all the time! Let's have a bit of peace and quiet please!

(GORDON turns off the television)

GORDON. Listen Tommy, I've been thinking –

TOMMY. That makes a change.

GORDON. I could do with help running the business. It doesn't take brains to be your own boss, you know?

TOMMY. You'd know.

BRENDA. Tommy, will you please stop it? Every other word Gordon says you contradict with something nasty or sarcastic! It's wearing me down! Please stop it.

GORDON. I've talked it over with your Mam.

BRENDA. There's not many options, son. Please think about what Gordon's offering, will you?

TOMMY. I shall in all my best obey you, Madam.

BRENDA. It's what your Dad would have wanted.

GHOST OF DAD. You always was a cheeky mare, Brenda.

TOMMY. It's not what I want.

GHOST OF DAD. That's right, son you tell him to stick his Tory principles where the sun doesn't shine.

BRENDA. What do you want?

TOMMY. I'm thinking of going into acting.

GORDON/DAD (mocking, simultaneous). *Acting??*

TOMMY. Yeah, you know – acting, like actors in films on the telly and plays in the theatre.

GHOST OFDAD. Acting's not a job!

GORDON. That doesn't sound very realistic, Tommy.

GHOST OF DAD. Welding, plumbing, carpentry, electrics, fitting, engineering - those are proper jobs, but not fuckin' actin'!

GORDON. Or practical – it's more a hobby, amateur dramatics and that.

GHOST OF DAD. Actin's for the fuckin' middle classes, lad!

GORDON. Don't you need something a bit more accessible?

BRENDA. Jobs don't grow on trees, Tommy. Gordon can start you at twenty-five pound a week.

GORDON. Youth Opportunities Program they call it, Tommy - special government scheme.

TOMMY. What's wrong with actin'?

GHOST OF DAD. You know perfectly well what's wrong with it!

GORDON. You won't find Humphrey Bogart down the Labour Exchange.

TOMMY. It's not called the Labour Exchange any more it's called the Job Centre.

GORDON. Changing the name of something doesn't change what it basically is, Tommy.

TOMMY. So sleeping in me Mam's bed and sitting at me Dad's table doesn't make you me Dad then does it?

GHOST OF DAD. Oh, nice one, son – you got him right in the bollocks there but hey actin's nae good for a working class lad, Tommy.

TOMMY. I'm good at it. The Drama Teacher says so.

GORDON. Look, you don't have to be a fishmonger if you don't want to, son.

TOMMY/DAD: I'm/He's not your son!

BRENDA. But there're no jobs for actors down the Job Centre, Tommy.

GORDON. It's about food on the table, bread in the mouth, some change in your pocket, a night out, some nice clothes and furniture, Tommy. It's not about piped-dreams.

TOMMY. They're not piped-dreams. They're *my* dreams!

(TOMMY exits in the huff)

GHOST OF DAD (to GORDON). See what you've done?

GORDON (to BRENDA). He's got your husband's temper.

BRENDA. You remind me of him sometimes.

GORDON. How's that?

BRENDA. We tell our kids to believe in their dreams and as soon as they do we tell them to stop being dreamers! What do you expect?

(Cue: 'New England' by Billy Bragg 'I don't want to change the world, I'm not looking for a New England, I'm just looking for another girl')

Act Two

1.

(JULIE'S house. JULIE, her Dad MR LOWES, 50's, and TOMMY sit drinking tea.)

MR LOWES. If you want to be an actor, be an actor, Tommy. I wish I'd had chances like that when I was a young man.

TOMMY. I'm not so sure. If my Dad was still about he might just agree with Gordon.

MR LOWES. I bet he'd be up at that Picket Line today, your Dad. But brave as they are, they wont last - if they had a ballot they'd all be back tomorrow.

TOMMY. We're going to win, aren't we?

MR LOWES. 'We'? Oh they like that word, the Tories, when what they really mean is 'me' But when was politics ever perfect? Do you know, there were more pits closed down under the last Labour Government than what even this lot have proposed? How quickly we forget. Last big strike in '72 the NUM brought down the government. I remember it well – power cuts and no water, everything brought to a standstill by the workers. Do you know, a billion of taxpayer's money goes into the coal industry to keep it propped up – *a billion quid!* You can buy a country for that! In China, Russia and South America they pay miners tuppence a day and tell 'em they can work, starve or in some cases get a bullet in the back of the head. You don't have to be Einstein to work it out. And now, to crown that piece of poetic prose, I shall retire to the lavatory and concentrate on images of Margaret Thatcher.

(MR LOWES exits with a newspaper under his arm.)

TOMMY. He's mad your Dad!

(JULIE kisses TOMMY on the mouth but he panics, worried about the father returning and pushes away.)

JULIE. What's the matter?

TOMMY. He might come back.

JULIE. I'm chucking myself at you and you don't want to know!

TOMMY. I do! I don't want - ! I just - !

JULIE. What? *What?* Are you a queer?

TOMMY. I don't know! How do you know if you're a queer anyway?

JULIE. It's all right if you are. I mean look at that Boy George and Freddie Mercury and George Michael from Wham.

TOMMY. George Michael's not a bender!

JULIE. Could have fooled me. Here, maybe you're a bi?

TOMMY. Buy what?

JULIE. A bisexual – you swing both ways.

TOMMY. I don't swing anything, anyway Julie! I just – I don't – I don't want to fuck it all up!

JULIE. I'll show you what to do. I've done it before.

TOMMY. Who with?

JULIE. Another lad.

TOMMY. Don't be a slag.

JULIE (she punches him hard, it hurts) I'm *not* a slag just coz I've had sex with another bloke, Tommy – you haven't got ownership rights! We're not living in the fucking Middles Ages anymore! You think you can have it all your own way! Well I can bump *and* dump nae bother and don't forget it!

TOMMY. Aye well I think maybe that's best.

JULIE. What do you mean – split up?

TOMMY. Yeah.

(It's a surprise to Julie and yet not a surprise at all when she thinks about if for a few seconds)

JULIE. All right.

TOMMY. I think it's better. We can still be friends.

113

JULIE. That's what people always say. And then they never talk to each other or see each other again for the rest of their lives.

TOMMY. I know. It's sad isn't it? But you want a baby and a career and I want -

JULIE. What do you want, Tommy?

TOMMY. Something different.

(A lavatory flushes. MR LOWES re-enters, smiling.)

MR LOWES. That's better – right between the eyes. Here, do you know Tommy there's a scab I know had his dog poisoned? His dog! What'd his dog ever do to hurt Scargill? Eee I don't know, whatever happened to the unity of the working class? Maybe it was always a myth? Even a Socialist paper like The Daily Mirror is against the strike! A classic smear campaign by the press! It divides communities.

(He throws down the paper in disgust)

JULIE (losing it). Oh give it a fucking rest, Dad, for God's sake!

(JULIE runs out, upset.)

MR LOWES. And it tears families apart.

(Cue: 'Girls Just Wanna Have Fun' by Cyndi Lauper 'The phone rings in the middle of the night, my father yells: 'What you gonna do with your life?' Oh Daddy dear you know you're still number one, but girls just wanna have fun'.)

2.

(Thunder. Rain pours. TOMMY waits for a bus, a newspaper over his head. PROSSER enters with an umbrella and shopping bag and sees TOMMY.)

PROSSER. Hello, Tommy – terrible weather. I can give you a lift home if you like?

TOMMY. No you're all right.

PROSSER. You're looking a bit down. A problem aired is a problem shared.

TOMMY. People do my fucking head in sometimes.

PROSSER. What people?

TOMMY. All of them - everyone just wants me to do really boring, stupid, pointless things: get a job, make money, have kids, get old. Is that all there is to it? Doesn't it get any better than that?

PROSSER. Getting a job, making money, having kids and getting old isn't boring or stupid or pointless, Tommy. It's just what some people choose and some other people have those choices made for them. But if you really want something it means you sometimes have to sacrifice certain things. You have to ask: what do I have to sacrifice to get what I want, and: do I really want to make that sacrifice? Listen Tommy, I know you might laugh but have you ever thought about auditioning for drama school in London?

TOMMY. What's that like, where you show them what you can do?

PROSSER. If they like you, you get to join them as a student and study to be professional and more than likely get you a good agent and after that you're laughing – next stop Hollywood, if Hollywood's what you want of course.

TOMMY. Aren't I a bit young at sixteen?

PROSSER. Technically, yes, but there's something about you Tommy Greaves, it's like you've been on this Earth before.

TOMMY. We could never afford it.

PROSSER. You can get a grant from the County Council. Taxpayer's money is put into free grants to help kids like –

TOMMY. Poor kids?

PROSSER. – like yourself.

TOMMY. They'd never have me – I'm rubbish.

PROSSER (stern). Don't say that, do you hear me? I don't teach idiots, Tommy Greaves. When I see a student respond to my teaching I feel good but rubbish yourself and you rubbish me and nobody rubbishes Barry Prosser.

TOMMY. All right, sorry.

PROSSER. They're not bothered about how rich or poor you are. You can walk tall and proud like Laurence Olivier or with the backs of your hands trailing the ground - like half the police on the picket line just now.

TOMMY. You support the miners don't you, Barry?

PROSSER. I support the principles, Tommy.

TOMMY. How do you mean?

PROSSER. We've got everything we need in this world – resources, brains, manpower – to create a world where one half looks after and respects and cares for the other half. This is the world our grandparents created after the second war. There's cohesion in that, a kind of glue that holds us all together. But this bitch Thatcher wants to melt that glue so that one half exploits the other half. I don't go along with that. I want to encourage potential, not exploit it. You've got potential, Tommy. I think you're good enough.

TOMMY. Nobody ever said I was good at anything.

PROSSER. Not even your Mam and Dad?

TOMMY. Not even them.

PROSSER. I could coach you. I'd do it for nothing.

TOMMY. Nobody does anything for nothing.

PROSSER. Money's useful but it's not all about money, there're principles as well.

TOMMY. You sound like Arthur Scargill.

PROSSER. I'd rather sound like Arthur Scargill than Maggie Thatcher.

TOMMY. Why?

PROSSER. Because it's about investing in people, not about rolling the dice or throwing dreams onto the wheel of fortune and saying: 'What will be, will be'. We've tried that since the dawn of Time and look at where it's got us: same place we started. We've got the resources to create a better world and what do we do with it? We pull ourselves apart with doubt because we suddenly realise just how courageous we'd have to actually be to make it happen.

TOMMY. You're funny you are.

PROSSER. Why do you say that?

TOMMY. That's another reason why you're not famous isn't it?

PROSSER. What do you mean?

TOMMY. Coz you get dead excited and passionate and I bet the last thing a Director wants on his set is somebody like you telling them how to do their job.

PROSSER. You can be an actor and a Socialist at the same time you know?

TOMMY. But can you though? You said I had to sacrifice so what if I sacrificed any kind of politics – Labour or Tory? Then I could do what the fuck I wanted and think what I wanted and not be beholden to anyone, right?

PROSSER. You're not as daft as you look are you Tommy?

TOMMY. You cheeky bastard! Here, can I ask you a question?

PROSSER. Fire away.

TOMMY. Are you a queer?

PROSSER. Ouch. Just when you were starting to turn from a caterpillar into a butterfly you turn into a Pleb instead.

TOMMY. You're not denying it.

PROSSER. It's none of your business what I am.

TOMMY. So you are then?

PROSSER. I'm not answering.

TOMMY. You wear a scarf round your neck – queers wear scarves round their necks like that.

PROSSER. Is that what you think this is about, a scarf around my neck?

TOMMY. Is that what *you* think this is about? I get free acting classes and you get to bum me off?

PROSSER. Tommy, don't talk like that, please. If you want to be a prisoner in a world of cliché that's your choice - you're just about old enough to make that choice.

TOMMY. All right. I'm sorry.

PROSSER. Will you think it over, about the drama school?

TOMMY. I already have.

PROSSER. And?

TOMMY. You know the answer. I've got to get the fuck out of here or it's going to kill me.

PROSSER. The Royal Shakespeare Company is coming to town in December. They're performing Hamlet. I think we should go and see them.

TOMMY. How much is it?

PROSSER. Never mind that. I'll sort it out and we'll drive up and then you can see it for yourself first hand. I've got some videos of Hamlet we can watch as well. The auditions are in the spring so you'll have to wait but we'll keep rehearsing. Deal?

TOMMY. Deal.

PROSSER. Don't let me down, Tommy.

(Cue: 'Stand Down Margaret' by The Beat 'I see no joy, I see only sorrow, I see no hope in your bright, new tomorrow so stand down Margaret stand down please, stand down Margaret'.)

3.

THATCHER'S VOICE: 'We had to fight the enemy without in the Falklands. We always have to be aware of the enemy within, which is much more difficult to fight and more dangerous to liberty. We have got an attempt to substitute the rule of the mob for the rule of law, and it must not succeed. It must *not* succeed. There are those who are using violence and intimidation to impose their will on others who do not want it. The rule of law must prevail over the rule of the mob.'

(Fade music. Sitting on a dustbin is TOMMY with ALAN, who has a Paisley scarf around his neck. From a bag ALAN shows TOMMY stolen goods: Parker Pens in their boxes, penknives, tape cassettes and videocassettes.)

ALAN. How much for these?

TOMMY. Nowt.

ALAN. I'm not selling this stuff for nowt, Tommy. There's twenty quid here at least.

TOMMY. No, that's not what I mean. I mean, I want to stop doing this, Alan. I want to stop buying knock-off and trying to flog it. It's not right.

ALAN. Since when did you get a conscience like?

TOMMY. I'm asking for trouble.

ALAN. I run risks as well you know, knocking this stuff? Fucking store detectives down Woolie's are right bastards – you have to be fucking bionic to outrun 'em.

TOMMY. Aye I know but handling stolen goods is as bad as nicking 'em in the first place.

ALAN. So what? You get caught, you get fined – nobody gets hung for thieving anymore, Tommy.

TOMMY. You get a fucking record, Alan. You get a record - you don't get a fucking job.

ALAN. You said you didn't want a fucking job. You said they could go fuck 'emselves far as you're concerned.

TOMMY. I know I did, but that was before.

ALAN. Before what?

TOMMY. Before the drama club.

ALAN. What's the fucking drama club got to do with anything?

TOMMY. This acting could be a way out for me. There's fuck-all else.

ALAN. Are you serious about it like?

TOMMY. The drama teacher thinks I should be.

ALAN. What's your Mam say?

TOMMY. She doesn't know. She doesn't give a fuck any road. Neither of 'em does.

ALAN. If they're anything like mine they'll say actin's for queers.

TOMMY. You do know only benders wear flowery scarves?

ALAN. Fuck off - blokes on the telly wear flowery scarves and nobody cares, like Kenny Everett.

TOMMY. Wearing flowery scarves is for queers, I'm telling you man.

ALAN. Your drama teacher wears a flowery scarf.

TOMMY. I know and I asked him if he was a bender.

ALAN. What did he say?

TOMMY. He didn't deny it.

ALAN (over macho). If you ask me if I'm a fucking bender I'll punch your fucking lights out. So what about all this gear?

TOMMY. This is the last time. I'm giving it up.

ALAN. That's your choice but don't expect me to join you.

(TOMMY gives him £20. ALAN exits. TOMMY gathers up the stolen goods, ensures ALAN has disappeared, lifts the lid of the dustbin and dumps everything in it. Cue: 'What Difference Does It Make?' 'The Devil will make work for idle hands to do, I stole and then I lied just because you asked me to but now you know the truth about me you won't seen me anymore but I'm still fond of you'.)

4.

(In darkness)

NEWSREADER'S REPORT: 'Almost three thousand more striking miners voted to return to work yesterday bringing the total to just over sixty thousand non-striking miners in a dispute that has now lasted nine months.'

(Fade music. Suddenly a loud explosion and then screams and moans and sirens)

VOICE-OVER MARGARET THATCHER: 'That is the scale of the outrage in which we have all shared, and the fact that we are gathered here now, shocked but composed, is a sign not only that this attack has failed, but that all attempts to destroy democracy by terrorism will fail.'

(Lights. GHOST OF DAD and TOMMY. TOMMY has a newspaper open to reveal the front page the day after the Brighton Bomb with the one-word caption

MURDER vertically down the right side so that the front and back covers open up like a broadsheet.)

TOMMY. Bloody hell. It's – it's unbelievable! It's like – like a bloody war zone out there – everywhere you go people shooting and blowing each other up.

(GHOST OF DAD opens a can of bitter)

TOMMY. You're drinking again.

GHOST OF DAD. Celebrating.

TOMMY. You're drinking.

GHOST OF DAD: I'm celebrating!

TOMMY. I thought you said ghosts couldn't drink?

GHOST OF DAD. We can't, not McEwans or Brown Ale. To the Irish!

TOMMY. What for?

GHOST OF DAD. Coz they almost succeeded in Brighton in doing what no Englishman could ever do: blowing the bitch to bits.

(DAD drinks. He offers it to TOMMY who shakes his head)

GHOST OF DAD. That bomb's been the one highlight of this whole rotten strike. Go on, 'ave a sip! All working men drink, Tommy, it's what we do.

(TOMMY tries to grab the can but his hand passes through it. He tries again and fails. GHOST OF DAD laughs.)

GHOST OF DAD. Ha ha 'Ghost Bitter - spirits for spirits!'

TOMMY. When you drank you beat up Mam.

GHOST OF DAD. You know how to put a damper on things don't you?

TOMMY. Strike's doomed if you ask me. Government doesn't give a fuck.

GHOST OF DAD. It's not just about coal, Tommy. It's about us and them.

TOMMY. But there is no 'us and them', Dad, there's just us.

GHOST OF DAD. Tories filling your head with propaganda, trying to persuade you to think like them.

TOMMY. Isn't that what you're doing? Trying to persuade me to think like you?

(TOMMY rummages in his holdall and finds what he's looking for, a big new Black & Decker claw hammer. He wraps it in the newspaper.)

GHOST OF DAD. What's that for?

TOMMY. I've found a home for it - George has invited me round for a Christmas drink. Are you coming?

GHOST OF DAD. No, I'm going down the Club to rub shoulders with some old mates.

TOMMY. Back to your old ways eh?

(GHOST OF DAD puts a fist close to TOMMY'S face to menace him)

GHOST OF DAD. Don't be fucking cheeky Tommy or I'll fucking smack you one!

(But TOMMY isn't intimidated and stands his ground without flinching)

TOMMY. No you won't because you're a fucking Ghost now and you're all hot air and you always were!

(GHOST OF DAD backs down – he has no choice, it's true, he is hot air. TOMMY packs his bag and exits. GHOST OF DAD is broken but as he used to do when he was alive, he coped with his rage by drinking. He thinks and exits. Cue: 'Do They Know Its Christmas?' by Band Aid.)

NEWS READER VOICE OVER: 'British Telecom shares will go on sale tomorrow to the general public in what is expected to the biggest share issue ever and should double the amount of shareholders in the United Kingdom. Weather-wise sub-zero temperatures and snow is expected across the north of England.'

5.

(GORDON and BRENDA around a decorated tree and plenty of food – unlike the miners that Christmas.)

BRENDA. I can't think why he could be so late.

GORDON. Down the pub probably with all the other wasters.

BRENDA. Well it is Christmas after all, no harm once in a while.

GORDON. I just hope he hasn't gotten himself arrested.

BRENDA. I was drinking at fourteen. Plastered loads of make up on and stuffed me bra with loo roll to get served.

GORDON. I bet you were a young temptress and no mistake.

BRENDA. I was that.

GORDON. Give us a kiss.

(She kisses him on the mouth and they embrace, a rare moment of tenderness between them. Enter TOMMY, a little drunk, holding a small cardboard box. He has a broken eggshell and yolk down his front and a bottle of milk in each pocket. He sees them kissing. They separate.)

GORDON. What did I tell you?

BRENDA. What's with the eggs and milk?

TOMMY. Egg fight.

BRENDA. You smell like a brewery.

TOMMY. I've had a few nips, it cannot be denied.

(He burps loudly)

BRENDA. I knew you'd end up like your Dad.

TOMMY. Give it a rest, woman – its Christmas, for fuck's sake! It might be the time of angels but we don't have to be one every day of the fucking week. (singing). 'Good king Wenceslas last looked out of his bedroom window, silly bugger he fell out on a red hot cinder, brightly shone his arse that night though the frost was cruel, when a poor man came in sight playing with his t-o-o-o-o-o-o-l !'

BRENDA. Please, Tommy, a bit of decorum – the neighbours.

TOMMY. Fuck 'em. Fuck everybody. Fuck the Tories. Fuck the Queen. Fuck the Pope. Fuck school. Fuck the BBC. Fuck Thatcher. Fuck Labour. Fuck Hamlet. Fuck Shakespeare and fuck fucking Santa Claus.

GORDON. Tommy, I – I got you a Christmas present.

(GORDON gives TOMMY an envelope. TOMMY opens it and takes out a letter and fails to read it)

TOMMY. What is it?

GORDON. Driving lessons. You'll have the chance to get about anywhere you want to look for work and do a few runabout jobs for me if you like.

BRENDA. And take your Mam to work sometimes and go for spins with your girlfriends.

(TOMMY ceremonially tears it up and throws the pieces into the air)

TOMMY. I told you: I'm not for sale. But let's not have any hard feelings at Christmas time, eh?

(TOMMY takes out a small gift-wrapped box but retains hold of it in his right/left hand. GORDON is stinging from the destroyed driving lessons but eager to keep the peace, he tries to take it.)

TOMMY. No, you have to open it like this while I hold it like so.

(TOMMY simulates the lifting of the four flaps of the top. GORDON unwraps the flaps as indicated and TOMMY'S free hand pushes up like a jack-in-the-box into GORDON'S face a two-fingered 'Fuck off')

TOMMY. Merry Christmas, Gordon!

(GORDON slaps TOMMY. TOMMY vomits behind the sofa. 'Wonderful Christmas Time' by Paul McCartney.)

6.

(In the black)

SCARGILL'S VOICE OVER: 'We've had riot shields, we've had riot gear, we've had police on horseback charging into our people, we've had people hit with truncheons and people kicked to the ground. The intimidation and the brutality that has been displayed are something reminiscent of a Latin American state.'

(Fade music. Lights. Sounds offstage of shouting, sirens and horses galloping on tarmac. TOMMY runs onstage out of breath followed by GEORGE. GEORGE displays a SUPPORT THE MINERS placard torn in half, his head bandaged.)

GEORGE. What the bloody hell do you think you're playing at?

TOMMY. What?

GEORGE. What the bloody hell do you think you're doing on the picket line?

TOMMY. If Dad was here he'd be up there today but he's not here so I am!

GEORGE. You're lucky you didn't get belted!

TOMMY. But we have to stand together!

GEORGE. What you're seeing up there isn't fit for the eyes of young men!

TOMMY. I'm fed up of hanging around doing nothing!

GEORGE. It's a battle of the Old Guard, Tommy! There's only two opponents: striking miners and Thatcher and her henchmen, but if you're not one and you're not the other – you stay out, you hear me?

TOMMY. I've got an opinion as well you know?

GEORGE. If your Dad was here he'd tell you exactly the same, Tommy!

TOMMY. I'm not my Dad – I'm me!

GEORGE. Listen to me, Tommy: when this is all over 'strike' will be a dirty word for generations! They'll be singing songs and making films about this bloody mess in years to come! This isn't a free-for-all riot between the rich and the poor, Tommy. This is a battle to the death!

TOMMY. But -!

GEORGE. And what about your mother? How would she feel if anything happened to you up there? How could I ever look your mother in the face again if anything happened to you, her only son? You stay away – it's nothing to do with you, you got me? Or do I have to punch you one meself to make you understand?

TOMMY. All right, George. I'm sorry.

GEORGE. Jesus, I'm out of breath. I'm too old for this caper.

(GEORGE sits down)

TOMMY. Some New Year this turned out to be eh?

GEORGE. Christmas wasn't so bad. Thanks for that hammer, kid.

TOMMY. Was it useful? I thought you might like it.

GEORGE. Used it pulling nails out of old furniture for the fire. Wish I could work out where all the other stuff came from though.

TOMMY. What other stuff?

GEORGE. Christmas morning when I opened the back door there was two packets of bacon, three pots of yoghurt, a gallon of milk and half a tray of eggs on the doorstep, all fresh. The milkman knew nowt about it and he didn't charge us for it neither. Me and the wife had a slap-up Christmas dinner.

TOMMY (sounding innocent). Maybe Santa's got a milk round?

GEORGE. If I ever found out who'd been following the milkman on his rounds at 6 o'clock in the morning stealing from other people's doorsteps I'd have words. Shouldn't be stealing from other working class homes.

TOMMY. How do you know it was nicked?

GEORGE. There were no price tags.

TOMMY. Maybe they were nicked from the big semi's up at the posh end of town, from them what can afford it?

GEORGE. If you know who nicked the dairy stuff, tell them not to do it again.

TOMMY. Will you go back on the picket line?

GEORGE. Not today. Oh fuck this for a game of soldiers. I think I'm going to take redundancy - that'll pay off the house. Retirement's only a few years away any way. It hasn't been so bad spending this summer of 1984 above ground instead of below it. Now don't forget what I said, Tommy. You go home now, do you hear? Promise me.

TOMMY. I promise, George.

(Enter GHOST OF DAD behind GEORGE. TOMMY sees him.)

GEORGE. You don't owe your Dad anything, Tommy. You don't owe anybody anything.

TOMMY. But if he'd been here he would have said something.

GEORGE. If I know your Dad he would have said the same as me: stay away. Oh Jesus, me head hurts. I'm going home.

(GEORGE exits)

GHOST OF DAD. Poor old George - he never was much of a fighter. But he's right about it not being your fight.

TOMMY. He's been good to me since you went and he's not always on the piss like you were.

GHOST OF DAD. What the fuck were you doing on the picket line?

TOMMY. How do you know I was on the picket line?

GHOST OF DAD. Come off it, Tommy – I'm a ghost for fuck's sake, I float around everywhere and see everything!

(Enter PROSSER)

TOMMY. Oh fuck.

GHOST OF DAD. Who's this?

TOMMY (to GHOST OF DAD). Barry the drama teacher – we were supposed to go to Newcastle to see a play.

PROSSER. I waited, Tommy.

TOMMY. I'm sorry, Barry.

PROSSER. I got the tickets and everything. You can't behave like that when you're a professional, Tommy - you won't last five minutes.

TOMMY (to BARRY) I wanted to picket.

PROSSER. You went on the picket line? But you're not even a miner!

TOMMY. I'm a miner's son.

GHOST OF DAD. You *were* a miner's son but I'm dead now so it doesn't matter any more.

TOMMY. But I wish I hadn't gone. It was horrible.

PROSSER. Who are you talking to, Tommy?

TOMMY. My Dad - the Ghost of my Dad.

PROSSER. The – the Ghost of your Dad? Where – where is he, Tommy?

TOMMY. He's everywhere, Barry. I see him everywhere, like he was here standing next to me. I hear his voice all the time and have conversations with him.

PROSSER. What does he say?

TOMMY. Stuff that makes sense to me, but then so do you and George and Brenda and even fucking Gordon.

GHOST OF DAD. Tell Barry what you saw.

TOMMY. I saw them grab a policeman separated from the other coppers. They pulled him around like a rag, kicking and punching him, his head bobbing backwards and forwards and side to side. He just – he just disappeared and they all just – like a pack of wild dogs ripping and tearing. Grown men, men with wives and children and mothers, fathers, sisters and brothers, loving, smiling, laughing, gentle men consumed by hate, overtaken by rage. Smoke from tear gas stinging me eyes and throat, I was shouting at the top of me lungs, 'Stop! Stop!' but none listening, none hearing, none making sense. I ran, Barry. I ran, Dad, as fast as I could, as far as I could. I tried to imagine being that copper's wife or father, mother, son or daughter visiting him in hospital, seeing that puffed-up, bruised face and bandaged head - my loving husband, my gentle son, my happy brother, my tender father, happy and smiling last time I'd seen them and now with these tubes leading out of him.

GHOST OF DAD. Don't go back on the picket, Tommy.

PROSSER. We've all got problems, Tommy, but home's home and work's work and this is our work, your work – the work of an actor.

TOMMY. What's in it for you, Barry?

PROSSER. All around I see talent going to waste – arts, poetry, science, sport. I see doubt and self-destruction - liberty imprisoned 'cause of Northern, macho traditions and the rich and the powerful down in London out of touch with the people who give them their wealth and power. And it's about London, Tommy, don't think you can live without it if you're going to be an actor in this country. You're going to have to cling on tight. But to break free you have to go against all you know - even when your friends are calling you a sell-out or saying 'So you think you think you're Mr Clever Clogs since you went off to London, do you?' and they will Tommy, oh they will.

TOMMY. They said that to you, didn't they?

137

PROSSER. Oh yes.

TOMMY. It's not they tell you you're crap. It's just – they don't tell you anything! And when you ask why they just say: 'Coz you're working class'. I feel like – like I'm talking treason to think differently to how me Dad thought. I feel like I'm just *pretending* - I've got everything I need: a home, a mother, a step-father offering me money and work, a girlfriend who wants to settle down but I keep thinking: 'There has to be more.'

PROSSER. There is more, much more - a whole world beyond your wildest dreams.

TOMMY. But who am I to dare to think I might be good at something nobody else is good at?

PROSSER. If you were no good, Tommy, we wouldn't be here now but you can't do that with just talk, you have to do it with actions – you have to go to London and you have to think: 'I tried. At least I tried. I can feel proud of trying.' Trying is more than most people do; it's what a few stubborn miners are doing right now: trying.

TOMMY. Have I really got what it takes, Barry?

PROSSER. Everybody wants to remember people and things that impress us - a song, a dance routine, a moment in a movie, a great laugh in a comedy – we all want to enjoy those moments coz they remind us all – the people doing them and the people enjoying them – that we're all just trying to make sense of life. You want to know the meaning of life? *That's* the meaning of life; the meaning of life is spending every second of that life trying to understand its meaning! I believe strangers who watch you act will feel the same way. You'll move them and remind them how they're just the same as you – no richer, no poorer, no smarter, no dumber – just the same and they'll remember you for that insight you gave them.

GHOST OF DAD. I'm not needed here.

(He goes to exit)

GHOST OF DAD. Stay out of trouble, Tommy and watch your back – with that flowery scarf he looks like a bit of a bender to me.

(Exit GHOST OF DAD. Enter DETECTIVE PALMER. He holds up a plastic bag with a brand new claw hammer visible inside.)

PALMER. Is this yours by any chance, Tommy Greaves?

(Cue: 'Life Shows No Mercy' by The Stranglers 'Everybody has some secret wishes, just keep your fingers crossed even if maybe they all come true, but don't worry if they just remain a fantasy, life shows no mercy'.)

7.

(TOMMY and DETECTIVE PALMER sit either side of a simple wooden table. On the table is the hammer.)

PALMER. A fishing rod goes missing. You're brought in for questioning. We can't hang nothing on you and let you go. An unwanted and unwarranted strike is loaded onto my shoulders. House burglaries increase – garden sheds broken into, tools stolen – petty thieving rockets as poverty sinks in. Shortly after *that*, you're seen selling stolen goods down the market.

TOMMY. Even though you've no witnesses.

PALMER. We've witnesses.

TOMMY. Yeah but then you lost 'em again when you started kicking them in on the Picket Line.

PALMER. One of those stolen goods is this hammer and you're seen on a picket line, of all the bloody daft stupid places to be.

TOMMY. I'm not denying it.

PALMER. Hammer hospitalises a Norfolk constable, married with a wife and child, who spent his Christmas on the critical list. I visited him - fair put me off me dinner.

TOMMY. I'm not to blame.

PALMER. Said hammer recovered from the scene at which you were present but despite our having taken your fingerprints, we can find no certain match.

TOMMY. No proof, no witnesses, no evidence.

PALMER. I can't believe I am sitting here pissing away my precious life on a yob. Why bother? You think I haven't got a million more important things to do than sit here wiping my arse on the likes of you?

TOMMY. So is this the part where you jump me and shove me head down the toilet bowl and force me to confess? I saw that episode of 'The Sweeney' as well, you know?

(PALMER reaches across the table, grabs TOMMY'S jumper, pushes him against the wall (or down on the floor) and starts slapping his face on every syllable.)

PALMER. This is the part where I say: 'You're free to go but with G-U-I-L-T-Y carved on your forehead with a plastic fucking fork you little cunt!'

(PALMER stops, allowing TOMMY to wriggle free, holding his neck, coughing.)

TOMMY. A hit, a very . . . palpable . . . hit . . .

(PALMER stops and unwinds)

PALMER: Oh God, this fucking strike!

(He relaxes, stands up, recovers his composure and straightens his shirt and tie.)

PALMER. Get up.

(TOMMY stands, straightens his shirt, tucks it into his pants, wipes the tears from his face)

PALMER. I don't ever want to see your face again. If I do – you'll be in a coffin and I'll be putting flowers on your grave. Now - fuck off.

(Cue music: 'Small Town Boy' by Bronski Beat 'Mother will never understand why you had to leave, but the answers you seek will never be found at home, the love that you need will never be found at home'. Lights down.)

8.

(In the darkness: NEWS REPORT VOICE-OVER: 'Newspaper allegations are now emerging that NUM leader Arthur Scargill has had contact with Libyan agents in Paris in searching for funds in order to continue the strike, this coming only nine months after the fatal shooting of PC Yvonne Fletcher outside their Embassy in London. Mr Scargill has vehemently denied such claims. More BBC news at six o'clock . . . '

(PROSSER and TOMMY. Tommy has a haversack.)

TOMMY. How much will it cost, drama school?

PROSSER. A few thousand.

TOMMY. Christ.

PROSSER. A year.

TOMMY. Fucking Nora.

PROSSER. For three years. Plus food and lodging but you can find a job to pay for that.

(TOMMY laughs)

TOMMY. Fucking hell, I might as well rob a fucking bank! Where am I going to find that sort of money?

PROSSER. There're grants from the County Council. Usually once the school accepts you it's a formality. What's with the bag?

TOMMY. I've left home. My step-dad and me don't get on. I've got nowhere to live. I was wondering –

(ALAN appears wearing only a dressing gown too big for him)

ALAN. Hello, Tommy.

TOMMY. Oh I see.

(TOMMY starts to leave)

PROSSER. Tommy, wait -

TOMMY. No, it's okay I get the picture.

PROSSER. I've got friends in London can help you out.

TOMMY. What, they put me up and what do they want in return, bend us over the sofa every night?

PROSSER. Why do you have to talk like that in that ugly, ignorant way? You'll be bumping into liberated men and women for the rest of your natural life – are you going to talk to all of them as if they were animals and not human because if you are you're not going to last five minutes in London.

TOMMY. I can't talk like you.

PROSSER. You've got talent, Tommy – it's just nobody ever told you. Nobody is this environment knows how to tell you that.

TOMMY. I see the sort of talent you're after.

ALAN. It's not like that, Tommy - Barry's looking after me.

TOMMY. Yeah I bet he is. It's fucking illegal what you're doing.

ALAN. We're not doing anything, Tommy! He's letting me stay, that's all. Anyway, what about Julie, can you not stop with her?

TOMMY. Julie wants to get up the spout and get a council flat.

PROSSER. Alan isn't staying forever, Tommy. You can have the sofa in a few weeks but it can never be permanent. I've got my own life to lead.

TOMMY. *I've - got - nowhere - to – live now,* Barry! Shall I spend the next nine months down the Sally Bash?

ALAN. Can't you make up with your step-Dad?

TOMMY. Oh fuck off, the pair of you's.

(He prepares to exit)

PROSSER. Will I still see you at rehearsal, Tommy?

TOMMY. Yes!

(Cue music scene change: 'Cruel Summer' by Bananarama 'Hot on the streets, the pavements are burning, I sit around. Trying to smile but the air is so heavy and dry. Strange voices are saying – what did they say? Things I can't understand. It's too close for comfort, this heat has got right out of hand'.)

9.

(TOMMY and GEORGE at the latter's home. They drink tea. GEORGE'S head is bandaged.)

GEORGE. So they booted you out?

TOMMY. I left. I had to.

GEORGE. Aye, I suppose. It happens to us all eventually. In the old days it was either that, marriage or the Army. Your Dad and me were down the pit at your age.

TOMMY. Did my Dad have dreams when he was my age, George?

GEORGE. Your Dad? Aye, he wanted to be a professional footballer. Play for Newcastle. He was a star at amateur Sunday League. Played for the town Youth Team.

TOMMY. I know he told me stories of goals he scored. Why didn't he do it?

GEORGE. Too much like hard work. And he came from a poor family, we all did – there was little time for the luxury of dreams. At school we only had to learn our ABC's and how to write our names. We were expected to leave at 15 and go straight into work. What else was there but the pit, like our fathers and our grandfathers? That was the way it was. We had no sense, no brains, no vision, no idea that life might offer us any more than what was in front of our noses. As soon as could, we got girlfriends and started drinking. Mind, we had some corker nights out though, the four of us, before you bairns came along. Day trips to Blackpool and Kiss-Me-Quick hats and fish and chips on windswept seafronts. We all four of us got married within a year of each other soon as we realised the lasses were pregnant - in my case my Lizzie with Mary and in your case your Mam, Brenda, with you. It's what you did in them days. Next thing you know you've an extra mouth to feed and no sleep at night. Then you're on the treadmill for life.

TOMMY. I've got to ask you something important, George.

GEORGE. Aye go on then.

TOMMY. You remember that hammer I gave you for Christmas?

GEORGE. Aye, you're not going to tell me it's nicked are you?

TOMMY. It might have been, aye.

GEORGE. Well it doesn't make any difference.

TOMMY. What do you mean?

GEORGE. I mean it had a hex on it that hammer - some bastard nicked it out me garden shed! Took a few tools they did, little bastards. People'll nick anything these days.

(TOMMY is visibly relieved as everything he was worried about suddenly makes sense)

GEORGE. Why do you ask?

TOMMY. Somebody hoyed it a copper on the picket line, put him in hospital.

GEORGE. Jesus Christ! The poor bastard.

TOMMY. The bizzies pulled me in for it yesterday, tried to hang it on me because I was on the picket line the same day the copper got it in his head.

GEORGE. What do you mean 'tried to hang it on you'?

TOMMY. It's all right, they've got no way of tying the hammer to me so whoever nicked it from your shed probably chucked it at the copper or gave it or sold it to someone who did. But there's a copper down there at the station's got it in for me – one foot out of line and I'm up the creek, George.

GEORGE. I see. So you want to stop here for a bit, do you? I'd have to speak to my wife. It's true we've a spare room since our Mary went off to Scotland. How long for?

TOMMY. Prosser the drama teacher thinks I've got a chance at this drama school in London. There's auditions in the spring but I need to apply now or I'll have to wait til 1986. A whole year and a bit hanging round this dump'll be the death of me.

GEORGE. Not good, kiddo, not good at all.

TOMMY. If I can get in this year I could start in September but I'd still have to figure out where to get the money from to pay for the training.

GEORGE. Training?

TOMMY. There's loads to learn: dancing, mime, stage-fighting, Shakespeare, improvisation, accent work.

GEORGE. You can get grants - that's how Mary's doing her college course. But we're not your parents, Tommy. And you've got no job and no dole, how can you eat?

TOMMY. I'll figure it out. Just a roof over my head for a few months'd give me a chance, George.

GEORGE. I owe it to your Dad I suppose but I can't have any shenanigans, Tommy - no thieving or drugs or parties or smoking or thumping music, I'm sorry but I can't - the wife's got angina. It's almost a year now without wages – a year! No strike pay - NUM won't sanction the strike and Thatcher's spiked the law so no dole neither. The jewellery's gone and if it weren't for Mary sending us money from Scotland we'd be in a right mess.

TOMMY. I just need a roof, George. I just need achance.

GEORGE. Either times are changing for the worst, Tommy, or I'm suddenly getting old. How it was different ten years ago: coal ran everything, without it the country ground to a halt. Now I'm out on strike for no good reason I can think of any more. I see those starving people in Ethiopia that that Irish feller Bob Geldof's singing about and I wonder: 'What have I got to complain of?' And this acting you're doing - what's that all about? I can't get me head around it – you of all people! Bloody hell. Well why not? But hey, before you get too comfy, you'd better figure out how to get your hands on some brass and you'd better do it legally, I don't want the bizzies round here and neither do you.

TOMMY. I'll work it out, George, I don't know how yet but I will.

(Cue: 'Shout' by Tears for Fears 'Those one-tracked minds that took you for a working boy, kiss them goodbye, you shouldn't have to jump for joy, you shouldn't have to jump for joy')

10.

(TOMMY and BRENDA at home)

TOMMY. I'm going to stop with George, Dad's old mate.

BRENDA. I know.

TOMMY. How do you know?

BRENDA. He came round last night and told me. Go back years me and George and Lizzie. We used to go dancing back in the 60's down the Palace when the bands used to come and play Beatle's songs. He'd not do anything that affected you without me knowing about it first.

TOMMY. I don't want to take Gordon's money.

(BRENDA opens her purse and puts a roll of a few hundred pounds on the table)

BRENDA. You won't have to.

TOMMY. What's this?

BRENDA. Six hundred and fifty, give or take.

TOMMY. Where'd you get all that?

BRENDA. The attic. All your Dad's stuff went up there after the funeral: electric shaver, gold wedding ring, cufflinks, old suits, silk ties, tie-pins, a big gold watch and chain from Victorian times and his blue suede shoes like Elvis – retro they call it these days. His punch bag, his bike, his record player, his rock and roll records by the boxful, 78's mostly and his prized possession: a signed football shirt by Bobby Moncur from his 1967 season at Newcastle United. In the old days men kept their money in portable wealth, Tommy, in family heirlooms.

TOMMY. All that was worth six hundred and fifty quid?

BRENDA. Four hundred – I've slipped an extra fifty in there from my own savings and after your Grandad died he left you a couple of hundred for when you got to eighteen but sixteen's close enough and you're seventeen soon. Now listen, giving you a big sum like that wouldn't be smart - you'd be broke in a week. So I've come to an arrangement with George to pay your bed and board upfront for nine months and then you're going to get a monthly allowance paid into your bank account by me. Those are the terms, Tommy – non-negotiable. It's an incentive to get to London 'cause if you don't, when that money runs out . . .

(TOMMY starts crying)

BRENDA. Hey! Here, stop that. Go to London, Tommy – do well. Make us proud. Make your Dad proud. Nobody in our family ever did anything like this. Tell them who you are and where you come from and don't be ashamed. Be proud like I'm proud of you.

(Cue: 'Relax' by FGTH 'We're shooting in the right direction, we're making it your intention, dream those dreams, scheme those schemes, gotta hit me (hit me) hit me (hit me) hit me with your laser beams'.)

151

11.

(The Audition Rehearsal. PROSSER, ALAN, GEORGE, JULIE, MR LOWES, MR WALLACE, BRENDA and GHOST OF DAD apart from the main group)

PROSSER. I've called you all here today as it's the last time Tommy and me will work on the audition speech before he goes off to London tomorrow so I thought it'd be a good experience so he gets a feel for what it'll be like in front of the people at the drama school. To think this young lad came to me a year ago with no idea what to do with his life and then watch him claw something back out of the despair, well it's been an inspiration, so lets hope Tommy can show the people down in London we might have lost the strike but we haven't lost our talent. Tommy . . .

TOMMY. To be or not to be, that *is* the question . . .

(Lights off on Tommy. A collage of images and the VOICE OVER work together in tandem. Images stretching from the Industrial Revolution and on to 1984-85: ink-drawings and black and white images of snot-nosed miner's kids, pit disasters, bleak streets and soup kitchens, cheap brick schools, Miner's Galas, black-faced underground workers, pit ponies, pit baths, derricks, coal wagons, chimneys pumping out smoke, furnaces, bridges and steel for ships in peacetime and war time, images of the 1984-85 strike, pickets, riots, fighting, protests, ambulances, injured men, wives and children in poverty and funeral corteges.)

VOICE OVER: The strike ended on 3rd March 1985, a year after it began. During the strike, eleven thousand people were arrested and eight thousand charged with offences such as breach of the peace, grievous bodily harm, assault and obstruction. The subsequent closure of pits affected engineering, railways, electricity and steel production, all linked to coal. Heavy engineering and manufacturing was slowly squeezed out of the British economy. Unemployment reached as high as 50% in some villages over the following decade.

(As the narrative goes on, those images are joined by those of closed factories and car scrap heaps, lines of unemployed men, Lech Walesa, the Fall of the Berlin Wall, Poll Tax Riots and anti-war protests in 2003.)

VOICE OVER. Gradually, Britain stopped producing products and started selling 'services' instead. But somebody has to produce products or the material world would fall apart. So what we did we do? We enslaved poor and uneducated people in other countries of the world instead of other parts of Britain by starving them of the information they needed to be unified and strong and paid them far less than any of us would ever dream of working for.

(Images now of vast rubbish tips inhabited by flocks of seagulls, swarms of children picking scraps, innumerable, teeming landscapes of Russian and Chinese miners carting mud or coal on their backs, starving people dying of malnutrition holding out begging bowls in slums, homeless on New York streets, refugee camps in nameless African states, riots suppressed by water cannon and tear gas, distraught stockbrokers as shares plunge on stock exchanges and vast icebergs break off and plunge into Arctic seas.)

VOICE OVER. The Miner's Strike, although its goals were not achieved, was one of those rare moments when a dying British breed known as 'the working class' rallied around the tattered flag of solidarity with other down-trodden workers from the shipyards of Gdansk to the steel mills of Pittsburgh. Pity those who were not with us for they will never understand what was lost by their absence.'

(Lights up on Tommy. He has his back to the audience - us. His audience – BRENDA, ALAN, PROSSER, MR WALLACE, MR LOWES, GEORGE and JULIE – stare, stunned with the finesse of what they've experienced. GHOST OF DAD is notably absent.)

TOMMY. And enterprises of great pith and moment with this regard their currents turn awry and lose the name of action.

(Cue: 'Don't You Forget About Me' by Simple Minds.)

(End)

Unspoken

I originally wrote this because I had a mixed-race French friend who lived in a rural village and told me Gendarmes had stopped her about twelve times over three years. By comparison I'd been stopped twice. She told me the police always used the same excuse: 'Your type of car is often targeted by thieves in this area' Of course, they would never say: 'Because you're black' - that would be racist. Another reason was how shocked I was that so many French villages have life-size crucifixes at their entrances and tackling this out dated concept seems to me to important – the worrying thing about humanity is how quickly we get used to something – good or bad - until we often reach a point where we don't notice it anymore and yet we can suddenly become defensive when outsiders coming into this environment criticise it.

Apart from the ballot box and anti-right-wing rallies, the French rarely use theatre to address these issues, unlike Britain with its long history of political theatre. So a combination of all these elements bubbling in my imagination came to the fore when I put these two opposing characters into the same space and time: the younger, open-minded, flexible, idealistic one up against the more mature, more experienced and more corrupt.

It was given a public reading in Paris with Marc Duret as CLAUDE and Cedric Vallet as JEANNE on Sunday 11th January 2015 – the evening of the afternoon of the rally for those murdered in the Charlie Hebdo massacre 5 days before. In 2018, JEAN, a man, became JEANNE, a woman, and new possibilities opened up for the story

Cast:
CLAUDE, overweight, late 40's. JEANNE, late 20's

Unspoken

1.

(Two French Gendarmes: CLAUDE, overweight, balding mid to late-40's and JEANNE, female, mid-20's - have set up a pair of digital binoculars on a tripod (traffic reduction camera) by the side of a country road. It is midday in June. JEANNE is looking through the binoculars. CLAUDE sets up a picnic table and two chairs, sits down on one of them on one side of the table and opens his lunch box. A speeding car passes.)

JEANNE: 47!

(CLAUDE brings out a napkin and ceremoniously tucks it into his blue shirt. Another car passes.)

JEANNE: 49! He's close.

CLAUDE: Have you eaten yet?

JEANNE: What?

CLAUDE: Have you eaten?

JEANNE: Yes.

(CLAUDE brings out a hunk of baguette and pate. He cuts the bread open with a clasp knife and spreads a little pate on it.)

CLAUDE: Pheasant – the pate. I shot it myself, the pheasant, not the pate. A wild one mind you, not one of these tame ones reared on a farm and released a few hours beforehand.

(Another car passes)

JEANNE: 48!

(CLAUDE eats)

CLAUDE: You sure I can't tempt you?

(Another speeding car passes)

JEANNE: . . . 52!

CLAUDE: Jeanne?

JEANNE: We could have had him.

CLAUDE: Jeanne!

JEANNE: We could have had him.

CLAUDE: It's lunchtime. Come.

(JEANNE pulls himself away from the tripod and sits, a little reluctantly)

CLAUDE: You know what the secret is?

JEANNE: What secret?

CLAUDE: The secret of the pate. The secret of the pate is to make the meat tender by basting it in its own fat during the roast. Without that fat, pheasant meat tastes like felt. Not that I know what felt tastes like.

(Another car approaches. JEANNE turns to the binoculars and as she does so, the engine of the speeding car rapidly decreases. CLAUDE doesn't even look up from his lunch.)

CLAUDE: You sure I can't tempt you?

JEANNE: Shouldn't I be hidden further down the road somewhere, Claude?

CLAUDE: You're stressing me, Jeanne. I can't eat when I'm stressed – bad for the digestion. Let me ask you a question: did you ride a scooter when you were younger?

JEANNE: A scooter? Yes. Why?

CLAUDE: How old were you?

JEANNE: 15, 16?

CLAUDE: Think back. Were you ever - out riding - one day somewhere - just maybe a little too fast?

JEANNE: Never. Sometimes.

CLAUDE: And if you saw a cop car, what did you do?

JEANNE: I slowed down.

CLAUDE: You slowed down. So, let me ask you this: what did you feel when you were saw the cop car by the side of the road, before or just after you slowed down? What did you feel?

JEANNE: Feel? Panic.

CLAUDE: Instant panic?

JEANNE: Yes, kind of. First - shock, then a kind of depression, then a kind of panic - all in a few seconds.

CLAUDE: Did they give you a ticket?

JEANNE: No.

CLAUDE: Did they pull you over?

JEANNE: No.

CLAUDE: What did they do?

JEANNE: Nothing.

CLAUDE: And what are we doing right now?

JEANNE: Nothing.

CLAUDE: Something.

JEANNE: Eating lunch, well, you are.

CLAUDE: Trying to.

(CLAUDE eats)

CLAUDE: After they saw you but didn't stop you and you felt panic and the panic subsided and you went on riding, what did you do next?

JEANNE: I made a point of staying under the limit for the next few days and remembering how lucky I was.

CLAUDE: And that's *exactly* what they're going to be doing for the next few days: counting their lucky stars.

JEANNE: I just thought we were supposed to be upholding the law is all.

CLAUDE: Dying to get stuck in, eh?

JEANNE: I just want to do a good job, Claude, that's all. I want to make the roads safe.

CLAUDE: Week two of a three-month trial period and already you're Dirty Harry, or Harriet. I know you want to do a good job. I know you want to impress me so that I write you a glowing report and send it up to Division.

JEANNE: I want to do what I'm paid to do.

CLAUDE: Well the first thing you've got to do is listen and the second thing you've got to do is learn: listen and learn. Are you listening?

JEANNE: Yeah.

CLAUDE: But are you learning?

JEANNE: I'm remembering what you tell me.

CLAUDE: Okay, so I'll tell you more: here's another example - the flash.

JEANNE: The flash?

CLAUDE: The flash. Flashing the lights. The signal. The warning. They all do it, right? They see us at the side of the road and they drive on past us and all the way they're flashing t the drivers on the other side heading our way, warning them.

JEANNE: Technically illegal.

CLAUDE: They know that, I know that. You know that. But illegal or not, they do it. Sometimes I'm off-duty driving the family car and somebody who doesn't know I'm a cop will flash *me,* and sure enough a few K down the road are some colleagues. But all I want to that day is go shopping. I can't be booking every one I see who breaks the law or I'd never get any shopping done.

So one way or another, whether we stand here looking through binoculars, whether we just sit here in our car or whether we know they're going to come slowly round the bend because other drivers have warned them – it's the same result, right?

(JEANNE pulls off a hunk of bread and eats)

CLAUDE: Were you a bad kid when you were young, Jeanne?

JEANNE: I wasn't bad. I was just a kid. Aren't we all at that age – clumsy, acting smart, over-cocky? They told me off a few times, the cops, when I was young.

CLAUDE: Do you know how many kids I've lectured in my career?

JEANNE: No.

CLAUDE: Too many to count.

JEANNE: It's just that at the Academy when it comes to classes on speed control they say: always be alert.

CLAUDE: The last time I was in the Academy, Mitterrand was President and we still had the franc. The Academy can teach you the rules, Jeanne; they can teach you self-defence, weapons training, high-speed pursuit and First-Aid. They can even teach you how to wipe your ass with your other hand. But they can't teach you experience. Nobody can teach you experience. Experience has to be learnt the hard way – out here.

(Another speeding car approaches. JEANNE turns CLAUDE touches his arm.)

CLAUDE: He's seen us.

(We hear the car's engine decrease speed)

CLAUDE: We don't even have to get up, see? Just to wear the uniform – the whole world pays attention. And you wouldn't believe what I've had offered over the years!

JEANNE: What, you mean bribes?

CLAUDE: And the rest - cash, contents of the boot, champagne, bottles of wine, caviar. Or they get nasty - tell me their husband's a lawyer, their cousin's the Mayor, they've friends in high places. Or they slip a hundred euro note in their Driving Licences and say it's accidental.

JEANNE: Have you ever accepted, a bribe I mean?

(CLAUDE winks and taps the side of his nose. Another speeding car approaches and passes)

JEANNE: 60! He was doing at least 60, camera or not!

CLAUDE: Forget it, its Jeanne-Christophe.

JEANNE: Who?

CLAUDE: Jeanne-Christophe – the Mayor. You'll meet him tomorrow as part of the getting-to-know-you routine.

JEANNE: But 60 in a built-up area and a primary school nearby?

CLAUDE: It's school holidays, Jeanne, where's the harm?

JEANNE: What do you mean?

CLAUDE: 'Selective Policing' I call it.

JEANNE: Speaks for itself.

CLAUDE: Plus he's President of the Hunt, President of *my* Hunt. Important man is JC - all over the place meeting people. He's already lost 9 points and we don't pay enough local council tax to hire him a chauffeur, so if you want to be the one that pushes him over the edge - be my guest. But can you imagine the tension tomorrow when we have to do the meet-and-greet and you've just handed him a one and hundred and thirty euro fine and screwed his licence for three years?

JEANNE: But it seems wrong.

CLAUDE: You've been here less than a fortnight, Jeanne. I'll see him tomorrow and have a word, that's all it takes.

(JEANNE doesn't speak but makes a clear 'What are you talking about?' gesture that CLAUDE can't ignore)

CLAUDE: What?

JEANNE: How do you tell the difference between the good guys and the bad guys?

CLAUDE: What do you do everyday, all the day? What are you trained to do from day one?

JEANNE: Be on my guard?

CLAUDE: You're trained to judge people. You're trained to look at anybody anywhere in the world, skin colour, how they dress, how they conduct themselves or move and make a rapid assessment and store away a little description up here (he taps his head) for future use. Immigrants, foreigners, thieves, druggies, pickpockets, students, hippies, travellers, queers, the poor in their crappy old cars and the well-off – like Jeanne-Christophe - in their nice new Mercedes. If I didn't know the Mayor of this village and President of the hunt drove that car, I'd book him, Jeanne. But I know he *does* drive that car, has nine points off his licence and one more conviction means he loses it. I can't un-learn that information can I?

JEANNE: No.

CLAUDE: How old are you, Jeanne? Twenty-four? My God, I was twenty-six when I started out a rookie while you were still in nappies.

JEANNE: I'd passed the nappy stage, just.

CLAUDE: I've learnt that you can't take on the world, Jeanne - you need to find a way to live with it and its faults.

Try this paté. Tell me what you think.

(JEANNE eats the paté)

JEANNE: I admit it's very good.

CLAUDE: See what your austerity is denying you? You must indulge, Jeanne, otherwise what are we here for? Tell me, do you hunt?

JEANNE: Not really.

CLAUDE: I never met a Gendarme that doesn't hunt. You're my first. Can you shoot straight?

JEANNE: I had a few good moments when I was in the Army.

CLAUDE: You were in the Army?

JEANNE: Three years. You look surprised?

CLAUDE: What were you in?

JEANNE: 8th Artillery, 7th Armoured out of Commercy.

CLAUDE: Me too - Signal Corps – 28th – Issoire. What was your rank?

JEANNE: Sergeant. You?

CLAUDE: Corporal. Blimey, I should be saluting you!

JEANNE: Forget it.

CLAUDE: Conscription got me – we had no choice in those days.

JEANNE: And no, I don't hunt. I can, but I don't.

CLAUDE: See any action?

JEANNE: Mali. I shot two-dozen enemy plant pots once.

CLAUDE: Two dozen what?

JEANNE: Red Cross, getting patients out of a hospital. Sporadic fire from kids with guns holed up in mud houses nearby. My job: shoot out the plant pots, that way the kids there knew they were being targeted and kept their heads down - just long enough to get the wounded to ambulances. That was damned fine shooting.

'Gendarme' seemed the obvious choice after demob, that or the Post Office. Could never see myself in yellow. Prefer my combat fatigues to the blue though!

What about you?

CLAUDE: Somebody had to stay at home and keep the machine running smoothly. I didn't mind volunteering. But a soldier who can take out two-dozen plant pots would be useful on a boar hunt.

JEANNE: But boars move, don't they?

CLAUDE: And how!

JEANNE: Not sure I want to shoot a rifle again at a boar or anything else.

CLAUDE: You carry a gun.

JEANNE: Because I have to.

CLAUDE: Hunting – you love it or you hate it. It brings out the primeval in a man. Instinct, it's always there inside us. No amount of legislation can iron it out. Sadly, nine times out of ten the people who live in cities, where there's no hunting, make the laws for people who live in the country, where there's the plenty. I'm not overly happy about that but sometimes the politicians in the cities have their uses. I guess it just depends which politicians, right?

JEANNE: Are there many boars in France?

CLAUDE: Too many. We're overrun. Draw a circle one kilometre long around where we're sitting now and you can dig out at least one.

JEANNE: I hear about them but never see them.

CLAUDE: Better that way. They keep their heads down if they know what's good for them.

JEANNE: You must know a lot about them?

CLAUDE: They run in packs, sometimes up to two-dozen, a couple of sows and generations of the same family, two or three families together 'til they get strong and then the males go solo. They hide out during the day in the one place they know we humans would never suspect – right under our noses and in the least obvious places, but they're there, tucked in hard and in a hard environment where we're not welcome, waiting. But if we try and go in there we need a suit of armour and a flamethrower. They know that. And they know we've lost half our menace when we're not on home territory.

JEANNE: They say you should run if confronted by a boar in the wild – is that tr7ue?

CLAUDE: Depends. If he's in pain he can be as afraid of you as you are of him. The most dangerous creature in the forest is a wounded boar.

JEANNE: The most dangerous creature in a war is a wounded man.

CLAUDE: A man with nothing to lose?

JEANNE: A man in a corner with nowhere to go.

CLAUDE: They'd be right. It's rare they kill people – boars that is - but they can maim and they can certainly kill the toughest hunting dogs.

JEANNE: I've had boar sausage and boar pate but I can't tell the difference myself - tastes like any other pork.

CLAUDE: Wild boars aren't castrated like factory-farmed pigs.

JEANNE: What's the difference?

CLAUDE: The taste - there's a commonly held belief that a castrated pig doesn't have boar taint.

JEANNE: Boar *what?*

CLAUDE: Boar taint - a certain odour that comes out in cooking, ruins the taste of the meat. Cut a pig's bollocks off and it'll produce good meat, but you can't cut a wild boar's bollocks off so you've got to take the risk shooting it. Sure, you can shoot a big boar but chances are he tastes like shit. Female meat is best they say and better to kill a female because then she can't reproduce. After a year the females start breeding and they can have five at a time in a litter. Imagine they have five female young each? In 5 years, that's five hundred - in five years! Only rats are worse. Just one female! Have you ever seen a boar up close, Jeanne?

JEANNE: It's just a tough little pig, right?

CLAUDE: It's more than that, it's a *prehistoric* tough little pig: primitive mentality, skin as thick as leather, legs like a bull, a metre high and maybe two long, short, tough legs, no neck – all muscle, all shoulders and chest a solid wall of weight and guts and two evil, yellow tusks either side of it's nose. Those are only little legs but when all four get to trotting at speed they can hit 50 in three seconds – just enough time to knock your legs from under you and stick you in your guts. You don't hunt a boar with buckshot - you hunt a boar with bullets. You hunt a boar like a soldier hunts the enemy. We have to keep their numbers down, Jeanne, if we don't – we'll be overrun. Sometimes I wonder what sport we could have catching these suicide bombers and letting them loose in a forest and hunting them down! At least they'd get a fair chance. What chance do women and children get in our shopping centres and underground trains and schools?

JEANNE: But you shoot deer as well. What harm can a deer do? You can buy venison in any shop, why kill them?

CLAUDE: Out here in the country we shoot to eat. We shop in supermarkets in the country as well, you know, we're not completely immune, we're not against, but we only do it because it's convenient and cheap. Daily food we get from local produce, farms, we grow, rear, hunt or fish. It pays to have a traditional outlook, Jeanne, to preserve the old ways. I shot the pheasant you're eating right now and it tastes good eh?

JEANNE: I'll give you that.

CLAUDE: Try the cheese.

JEANNE: What is it, a blue?

CLAUDE: From the Auvergne.

(JEANNE tries little piece and eats)

JEANNE: It's rich and creamy. Did you make that?

CLAUDE: No, the wife's cousin. What do you have in that lunchbox of yours?

(Jeanne opens his lunchbox)

JEANNE: A ham and cheese baguette, strawberry yoghurt and an apple.

CLAUDE: Let me see.

(CLAUDE looks inside)

CLAUDE: Super U?

JEANNE: My husband's working, we haven't always got time.

CLAUDE: Super U has its uses but Super U isn't the taste of France – it's the taste of bland Europe.

JEANNE: No but it's easy to pop in the shopping basket, reasonably tasty and if you haven't eaten for hours you'll eat anything.

CLAUDE: You'll learn country ways, Jeanne. You'll have to if you're going to stay.

JEANNE: Maybe I'm not.

CLAUDE: Oh?

JEANNE: I thought it'd be good to break myself in here and when I've got a couple of years under my belt, look for a position in a big town. In big towns there's some challenging work.

CLAUDE: Ah! She's ambitious! She's going to save the world! We've our challenges out here too you know?

JEANNE: Yeah? Ok then, what was the last incident you investigated?

CLAUDE: Here? Stolen bicycle.

JEANNE: Stolen bicycle? Did you find it?

CLAUDE. It'll on be for sale on the black markets of every country in Europe by tea-time.

JEANNE: What about round here? What happens round here?

CLAUDE: Drunk and disorderly, domestics, traffic stuff: drink driving, speeding.

JEANNE: So if I want to pull a vehicle that's suspicious what would I have to say?

CLAUDE: You'd have to ask: why is it suspicious? Is there something about the driver bothers you? Or about the car or the way it's being driven?

JEANNE: But you need a reason to stop somebody, right?

(CLAUDE shrugs)

CLAUDE: Not really. You're a gendarme – you can say what you want. 'Type of vehicle' is what I normally say.

JEANNE: What's that?

CLAUDE: 'I've pulled you over because we've recently had reports of this type of vehicle being stolen.' That way they don't suspect you're pulling them over for any other reason.

JEANNE: What other reason could you have for pulling them over?

CLAUDE: There may be something wrong with the vehicle or it may be being driven erratically or there's something suspicious about the driver. It's your call. You are the law. You make the judgement. You said you'd been married three years - what does he do, your husband?

JEANNE: Primary school teacher.

CLAUDE: Two civil servants? You can look forward to a comfortable and early retirement.

(CLAUDE produces a photo from his wallet. JEANNE looks briefly and smiles.)

CLAUDE: You don't carry a photo of your husband with you?

JEANNE: No.

CLAUDE: Hm. Cousin of hers up from the Dordogne cooked us woodcock last night! Woodcock – can you believe it? I'd never tasted it. And how it was cooked! Hung by its neck over the wood embers of the fire for an hour, just gently turned this way and that by the string. He put a bowl underneath to catch all the shit and guts that ran out. The meat was fat and rich, just lifted off the bone. All washed down with a sweet white. They know their birds down there. And you, what did you eat last night?

JEANNE: Salad, steak, bread from the Artisan baker and spring water.

CLAUDE: Spring water? Christ, what are you, a monk?

JEANNE: Not a fan of drinking. My father was over fond of it. Cirrhosis got him in the end.

CLAUDE: Policemen aren't what they used to be in the old days. Why did you join the service, Jeanne?

JEANNE: To protect people.

CLAUDE: Against what?

JEANNE: Crime, bad people. To protect people who can't always stand up for themselves. Isn't that why most of us join?

CLAUDE: I joined because the money was good, and the pension. The Army and the service – there's a certain order to things I like. But these 'bad people' you talk about, how do you know who these bad people are?

JEANNE: I was hoping you'd teach me.

CLAUDE: Then you have to ask yourself a question: are people essentially good or essentially bad?

JEANNE: I think they're all good but once in a while the temptation to be bad comes along and the good ones fall to the left and the bad ones fall to the right.

CLAUDE: And when they fall to the right, you'll be there to catch them?

JEANNE: I'll be there to arrest them.

CLAUDE: You know how I deal with it?

JEANNE: Tell me.

CLAUDE: They're all bad people. We're all bad people. Laws are made to try to temper the badness in us.

JEANNE: In the old days they used to think crime was a disease.

CLAUDE: Crime *is* a disease.

JEANNE: Now this is where our views differ: for me poverty is a disease and ignorance is a disease and these two things make crime. Look at the two parts of any town: on one side the detached houses with big gardens, nice cars in the driveways, educated families with good jobs and nice incomes. Do we get any crime there? No. Okay, sometimes a spoilt kid crashes his father's car. On the other side of the town there's HLM and how often are police called there for drugs, vandalism, domestic violence and mugging?

CLAUDE: And what other element, apart from ignorance and poverty, has this breeding ground got? I tell you what: it's as plain as the nose on your face and I'm not racist, Jeanne, everybody who knows me will swear to you I'm not racist, but is it any coincidence all the foreigners live there, with their menial jobs or no jobs and no understanding of French life? And what do they do with the civilization we give to them? Do they build schools and businesses to educate and feed themselves? No, they get out their prayer mats and say Allah wills it.

JEANNE: If Allah is their God, they might say that. But poverty is the fault of the government, not us. We exist to clean up the government's mistakes. It's nothing to do with God, it's to do with poverty and racism and lack of opportunities.

CLAUDE: If only life was so simple! Who did you vote for last general election?

JEANNE: That's a personal question.

CLAUDE: Asking who you vote for, what is there to be ashamed of in that? You want to hide so you can switch sides without having to defend decisions?

JEANNE: I didn't say I was hiding or wanted to switch sides. I just think it's personal. Why, who did you vote for?

CLAUDE: Le Pen.

JEANNE: Le Pen?

CLAUDE: Why not? I told you: sometimes the politicians do good things, *sometimes*. Locally, I'm middle of the road, sometimes Left, once I even voted Green – but I think I was a little drunk. European and Nationals - vote Right every time. The Euro MP's hold the keys to the doors of Europe and France, Jeanne. They decide who comes in and who stays out.

JEANNE: But the FN?

CLAUDE: Look around you, my young friend – we've learn to be tolerant.

JEANNE: If we had tolerance there'd be no Le Pen!

CLAUDE: Is this village riddled with crime? Do you see suicide bombers? Do you see drug addicts? Do you see rapists? Do you see gangsters and pimps? No, you don't. Because people like me with some courage, some sense of tradition, vote for the FN so at the highest level, up there in Parliament and more importantly in Brussels, they can create laws that nip extreme views in the bud before they blossom. Brussels is where it counts, Jeanne:

keep extreme views out of France. And if they should make it through the sieve, the last line of defence is us.

JEANNE: You, Claude, not 'us'. Those are your views, not mine. I work from the basis that we're all fundamentally decent.

CLAUDE: Which is why the law must be strong and firm – to bolster such naivety.

JEANNE: How can the law be strong and firm if you don't give the Mayor a ticket because he's president of your local hunting club?

CLAUDE: This is why I urge you to find a way to live with it, live with yourself and most importantly, live with your colleagues.

(JEANNE'S phone rings. The voice gives details of something only JEANNE can hear. CLAUDE picks his teeth with a toothpick. JEANNES finds a notebook and pen and writes something down. She ends the call.)

CLAUDE: Well?

JEANNE: There's been a crime.

CLAUDE: Is it serious?

JEANNE: You're the expert.

(End of 1)

2.

(On the stage laid on its back but at an angle, against a small grass bank that curls round in a semi-circle behind where it once stood, is a life-size wooden red-painted crucifix with a faded Bakelite statue of the white-skinned Christ figure nailed to it, red paint on its hands and feet. The facial features are life-like but faded. The crucifix has been chopped off at the wooden base, the stump remaining upright in the ground nearby, cordoned off across the front by a rusty chain. JEANNE and CLAUDE both speak on separate mobile phones, each side of the monument. Both say goodbye to their callers and ring off, CLAUDE first followed by JEANNE a few seconds later.)

CLAUDE: That was the Mayor.

JEANNE: Did you mention the speed limit?

CLAUDE: I didn't need to - he said he saw us, asks us to forgive him - he was late for a meeting. What did the journalist say?

JEANNE: I told her we'd answer when we had more facts.

CLAUDE: What she publishes may have a negative effect on the image of the village, on tourism too. I can't believe somebody would do such a thing. What is the world coming to?

JEANNE: When did you last see it standing?

CLAUDE (thinks): Yesterday, I think. Yes, yesterday. But you know I think I stopped looking twenty years ago - it was a fixture.

JEANNE: I've seen these in lots of villages around here.

CLAUDE: France is a catholic country, what do you expect?

JEANNE; France is a multi-faith country. We've got all denominations here now.

I just wonder how I'd feel if I was a Muslim or a Jew and saw this staring down at me? Would I feel welcome? Would I feel this was a place I'd want to settle and raise my children? I mean, that's what we tell city people, isn't it? 'Don't raise your kids in violent cities full of crime - go and live in a nice picturesque little French village!' I wouldn't mind chopping all of these down myself to be honest. They're out of date.

CLAUDE: Out of date or not, it's an act of vandalism and vandalism of public property is a crime. First we need to establish what time it was done.

JEANNE: And how. How long has it been standing?

CLAUDE: Type of wood?

(JEANNE goes closer to stump and examines it)

JEANNE: Oak. It was creosoted once but hasn't been re-treated in a good long while by the looks of it, sitting out here in freezing winters and roasting summers has burned it away, made the surface solid.

Most people walk or drive past this a hundred times a day and never have any reason whatsoever to cross the little chain and touch the base of the crucifix, do they?

CLAUDE: People of a religious frame of mind.

JEANNE: We agree it was chopped?

CLAUDE: What if he was wearing gloves?

JEANNE: Or she? An axe?

(CLAUDE steps closer to the base of the crucifix)

JEANNE: Careful where you put your feet, Claude – prints, shoe soles.

(CLAUDE examines the stump of the crucifix)

JEANNE: Yes, definitely an axe. Multiple blows.

CLAUDE: Sharp or blunt?

JEANNE: Sharp and not in one attempt.

CLAUDE: What do you mean?

JEANNE: The noise. This isn't a busy road – one or two vehicles every few minutes. Where's the nearest residence?

CLAUDE: Mrs Forrester's over there.

JEANNE: We should ask her if she saw or heard anything. I can do that. Have you got the camera?

(CLAUDE brings a camera out of his jacket pocket and walks around photographing everything)

JEANNE: The marks on the stump - some are fresh but some are quite old. The colour of the wood and all the blows have been dealt from the back, behind the pole.

CLAUDE: So?

JEANNE: This wasn't done in one go - it was done over a period of time so as to hide the marks from pedestrians.

CLAUDE: Which suggests?

JEANNE: Random acts usually burn themselves out quickly, but whoever did this came back a number of times over a period of time.

CLAUDE: What would Sherlock Holmes say?

JEANNE: He'd probably say: 'What's the motivation?'

CLAUDE: And your opinion?

JEANNE: Somebody with a gripe against the world?

CLAUDE: Somebody with a gripe against Father Martin?

JEANNE: Somebody with a gripe against the Town Hall?

CLAUDE: Somebody with a gripe against religion?

JEANNE: Maybe whoever did it was in a car or on a bike? I mean it's an isolated spot. How would they hack it a few times every now and again and get away without being seen?

CLAUDE: Maybe they did it at night?

JEANNE: Maybe. Or maybe if anybody saw them they presumed that that somebody was part of the natural landscape.

CLAUDE: There's a lot of 'maybe's' in your theory.

JEANNE: Well, a jogger, for example, a farmer in the field, some guy from the council emptying the litter bin, somebody driving a van that looked like it was from the council. Any white van with a red stripe looks official.

CLAUDE: What would be their motivation?

JEANNE: Somebody who disliked religion, or somebody trying to communicate something else to us?

CLAUDE: But if they disliked religion, why pick on this religion? Somebody who doesn't like Catholics or Catholicism?

JEANNE: Who doesn't like Catholicism enough to chop down a crucifix? If I don't like something I tend to just ignore it. Why bother to go this end, taking such a risk?

CLAUDE: A Muslim?

JEANNE: Are there any Muslim's hereabouts?

CLAUDE: Family from Paris moved in about six months ago: father, wife and two teenage sons: one 13 and still in college, the other, 18, unemployed and thinks he's a hit with the local girls. I saw my daughter Rosie chatting to him one day near the Bus Shelter. Asked her afterwards - she told me: Ahmed she said his name was. Then there's your anti-Christian element.

JEANNE: You think maybe Al-Qieda ordered a Jihadi cell to come out here into the middle of rural France to chop it down?

CLAUDE: I'm just saying at this stage all theories have to be considered. It pays to know who and where everyone is. We've got Catholics, Protestants, Jews, Christians, Buddhists, Muslims, Druids, Atheists and Agnostics. Plenty to choose from but motives is what separate the wheat from the chaff, motives.

(CLAUDE takes out a notebook and writes)

CLAUDE: So – facts: probably a male but possibly a female?

JEANNE: Male - it'd take some considerable arm strength to chop through this age of oak. Looking at the angle of entry I'd say it was a sharp blade and a short one – the cuts aren't very wide, six centimetres at most, but quite clean. I could ask at the local DIY store and see if anybody bought an axe recently?

CLAUDE: Dozens of people buy axes for chopping firewood in the country and how recently is recently?

JEANNE: Let's say the last eighteen hours - that'd take us back to about six yesterday evening.

CLAUDE: That's when I saw it standing.

JEANNE: We could put a notice up asking for witnesses and a hotline number?

CLAUDE: Take a while to get a response.

JEANNE: If we can narrow it down to a certain time scale then we can pull in suspects and find out their whereabouts and see if their alibis are sound. But kind of embarrassing though isn't it?

CLAUDE: What is?

JEANNE: Not knowing who was the last person to see it standing and when?

CLAUDE: Well, like I said, I drove past it yesterday evening and Father Martin must have seen it because he noticed it was down.

JEANNE: Well-attended his masses are they?

CLAUDE: Dwindling I'd say. Funerals and marriages – marriages because there's free booze and funerals are a chance to catch up on gossip. But ask them to attend regular Sunday mass and they've got a million excuses to be somewhere else.

JEANNE: Are you a churchgoer, Claude?

CLAUDE: I doubt you are.

JEANNE: I don't just dislike one religion over another - I dislike them all. But we live in a tolerant society, so – I tolerate.

CLAUDE: I'm working with a heretic. So, we've got a male – local - somebody who passes this way regularly – or: a random driver feeling angry and seeing an easy target?

JEANNE: I'd say local.

CLAUDE: Why?

JEANNE: Just to be aware of the routines so as not to be noticed.

CLAUDE: Well that narrows it down to about two thousand suspects. However, if their motivation is anti-religious that would narrow it down to about half a dozen.

JEANNE: How's that?

CLAUDE: Put two and two together.

JEANNE: You're suggesting questioning your Muslim family?

CLAUDE: They come from Paris - St Denis. I don't know anybody in this village that comes from St Denis. What did they do to make them leave St Denis and come out here? Is the kid selling drugs? All the kids in St Denis are on drugs or selling drugs.

JEANNE: Not all kids are on drugs. So he gets stoned one day and decides to chop down a local crucifix? Picking on an Arab Muslim kid because he comes from St Denis is a bit of a long shot without hard evidence.

CLAUDE: We're police – we don't need hard evidence. We play hunches. I've been playing hunches for twenty years longer than you have and hunches have served me well.

JEANNE: Why not write it off?

CLAUDE: Write what off?

JEANNE: Forget it.

CLAUDE: Forget it? Why?

JEANNE: You were keen to forget the driver who broke the speed limit.

CLAUDE: That was different.

JEANNE: I can't see how. You're saying there's one law for one and a different law for another and the person that makes that decision is the Gendarme.

CLAUDE: You're passionate about it. I respect that, Jeanne. Most young people are passionate about things. It's us old-timers who get a bit jaded.

JEANNE: Whoever did this probably knew they were going to get away with it, that's why they did it. Somebody graffiti's the local bus stop - we don't waste time trying to figure out who did it, we just give it a paint job and start again.

CLAUDE: There's a principle at stake.

JEANNE: There's a principle at stake when you turn a blind eye to speeding motorists because they're your wife's second cousin or whatever.

CLAUDE: What are visitors to this town going to think of us if there's nothing but a stump standing there? What are residents of this town going to think of its local police force if they can't protect something like a public monument? If this were a Muslim monument there'd be riots in the streets.

JEANNE: Muslims don't go in for that sort of thing, representation of their God in statues, so that comparison holds no water.

CLAUDE: That doesn't mean they're right. So, here's what you do: you knock on some local doors and ask if anybody has seen anything suspicious recently. I'll question some suspects too and then we'll meet back at the station and compare notes.

JEANNE: Okay. What about this?

(She indicates the broken monument on the ground)

CLAUDE: Down the tip.

(End of 2)

3.

(The police station. The crucifix is propped against a wall. CLAUDE has hung his jacket over its head as a convenient coat hook. CLAUDE prepares his evening meal, setting the table for two. JEANNE enters.)

CLAUDE: The *foies gras* is from my cousin: rolled in crushed peppercorns while maturing to give it that little kick on the tongue, but not burning like chilli or curry. The bread - we call it 'une vigneronne' made from walnuts, raisins and black Sarassin flour.

(JEANNE pulls off a piece of bread and uses it to scoop a little foie gras which she then eats)

CLAUDE: Verdict?

JEANNE: Very good.

CLAUDE: Isn't it? The taste of true France - you can't buy that in a supermarket. So, now, down to business: how did it go?

JEANNE: I met a lot of people.

CLAUDE: I bet you did. How many offered you drinks?

JEANNE: Quite a few.

CLAUDE: And how many did you accept?

JEANNE: None, of course.

CLAUDE: The mark of a young professional. I was the same when I was your age – full of zeal. What happened? I said yes one day! How many houses?

JEANNE: Ten. It's a lot or not enough?

CLAUDE: Eager. So you met all the neighbours within a five hundred-metre radius of the crime scene?

JEANNE: Not all – three weren't home and one is a holiday home.

CLAUDE: Yes – a retired English couple. They come here once a year in the summer and leave the place empty the rest. Waste of a lovely house if you ask me. How many young French couples would die for a starter home like that? Instead it sits there empty eleven months of the year - absentee landlords. But they pay their bills and their taxes so for this we must forgive them.

JEANNE: You don't like them?

CLAUDE: I didn't say that. The English are like a rash – they get everywhere. Worst is they mix with their own. They can't or don't want to learn our language or integrate or learn our ways. So we ignore them, push them out on the edge of the circle of tolerance. I keep an eye on their property. So you spoke to six residents, is that right?

(JEANNE gets out his notebook and reads)

JEANNE: Monsieur Beaumatin, Madame Gerard, Monsieur et Madame Menard, Monsieur Marchand and Mademoiselle Ferret.

CLAUDE: Jack, Marie-Pierre, Gaspard and Pascale, Phillipe and Minette.

JEANNE: You know them all?

CLAUDE: You have to get to know your way around. What did they tell you?

JEANNE: Mr Beaumatin wasn't in town yesterday - he was visiting his sister in Rennes.

CLAUDE: Lulu - 96 if she's a day - hanging on for dear life she is, but when he inherits he'll be the richest man in town.

JEANNE: Madame Gerard was home all day but taking care of her grand children and doesn't remember seeing or hearing anything unusual, plus the fact her house is hidden from the road by the garden. And she asked me to say 'Is it good?'

CLAUDE: Is what good?

(JEANNE produces a bottle of Bordeaux that he puts on the table. CLAUDE looks at the label.)

CLAUDE: Oh it'll be very good, knowing their cellar.

JEANNE: Mr and Mrs Menard said they were entertaining guests, I asked their names and they gave them as 'Marc and Lydie' but said they didn't know their surnames, which I found a bit odd. Said they came from La Rochelle. I asked where in La Rochelle but they wouldn't say but they swore this 'Mark and Lydie' were at their home all yesterday morning, afternoon, evening and night. Bit strange don't you think, not to know their surnames but to spend an intimate weekend with them?

CLAUDE: Wife-swappers.

JEANNE: What?

CLAUDE: They're wife-swappers. Ten to one they were entertaining.

JEANNE: How do you know that?

CLAUDE: I've seen it.

JEANNE: You've ... seen it?

CLAUDE: Between me, you and him (he indicates the crucifix) a few years ago I got a tip somebody had seen a naked stranger walking round the garden. So I went and had a discreet peek through their blinds and saw it all.

JEANNE: What did you see?

CLAUDE: Stuff they don't tell you about in the Bible. It's not my cup of tea but each to their own. Next.

JEANNE: Mr Marchand was very forthcoming: said he was an old friend of yours, asked how you were etcetera.

CLAUDE: We hunt together.

JEANNE: Said he saw a number of suspicious people in recent days but when I asked for details about makes of car or clothes he was scant on detail but just said they were all either black or Arab. He didn't use the words 'Arab' or 'black' - he referred to them as 'camel shaggers' and 'monkeys'.

CLAUDE: Philippe is our local National Front candidate.

JEANNE: You vote for him?

CLAUDE: We hunt together that's all. And Minette? Mademoiselle Ferret?

JEANNE: She was in Ancenis all day with her boyfriend and came home very late so she has a good alibi.

CLAUDE: A very good alibi – her boyfriend is my son. So who are your suspects?

JEANNE: I don't seem to have any.

CLAUDE: But a useful get-to-know-the neighbours exercise isn't it?

JEANNE: Or a waste of time. What about you?

CLAUDE: I think I found him.

JEANNE: What, you found the culprit?

CLAUDE: Oh yes.

JEANNE: Who? Where?

CLAUDE: His family don't know where he is just now – haven't seen him for at least two days they said.

194

JEANNE: Who said?

CLAUDE: The Hadids.

JEANNE: Who are the Hadids?

CLAUDE: Go figure. I asked where their eldest is and they didn't know. Said he likes to off on his own sometimes. Said he likes being out in the countryside, can't help it, they said, loves the freedom and the fresh air after years in the smelly city.

JEANNE: When you told him about the chopped–down crucifix, what did he say? How did he react?

CLAUDE: 'My boy would not do such a thing – I brought him up to respect the property of others' I said: 'Well, judging from his previous convictions and his attitude towards public telephone boxes I'd say you didn't do a very good job.'

JEANNE: Has he got any previous?

CLAUDE: I ran a check: drunk and disorderly and vandalism.

JEANNE: Oh?

CLAUDE: Paris, two years ago - some party got out of hand and he smashed up a 'phone booth.

JEANNE: I thought Muslims don't drink?

CLAUDE: Black sheep apparently.

JEANNE: Did you ask if they could provide an alibi?

CLAUDE: And there's the thing – he couldn't give me one. Just told me since leaving St Denis his boy had discovered the countryside and nature and all he did everyday was go for long walks. Bravo, said I, but it's what he gets up to on those long walks concerns me. 'Takes long reflective walks along the river' they said.

JEANNE: Where is his local mosque?

CLAUDE: Nantes has the nearest.

JEANNE: That's quite a hike. Does he drive?

CLAUDE: Scooter.

JEANNE: That's quite a scoot. But one previous two years ago and the fact that he's not around just now is hardly strong evidence to charge him. Maybe we should just write it off?

CLAUDE: A religious monument, the pride of the village, publicly desecrated and the local police force does nothing about it?

JEANNE: Well Claude, isn't it like what you said: when we're spotting speeders our presence keeps crime down, not so much that we actually stop and book offenders? And anyway who says it's the pride of the village?

CLAUDE: Somewhere right now somebody is walking round feeling invulnerable because he thinks he got away with it. And if he gets away with this, maybe he'll do it again? Maybe he'll go out and do it to another local village? And maybe one night burn down the local church? I'd like to watch you tell Father Martin we had a suspect in our sights but we decided to write it off.

JEANNE: But you can't pick up this Muslim family and single out their teenage son who likes to take long walks in the countryside without hard evidence, Claude.

CLAUDE: We can get the evidence under questioning. That's why we need to find him and find out what he's been up to recently.

JEANNE: What about a search warrant?

CLAUDE: For what?

JEANNE: A chopping axe?

CLAUDE: I told you: we live in the country – there's a million chopping axes. No, we keep our eyes and ears open. We tell the Town Hall, priest and the journalist we're looking for suspects and the case will remain open – standard line.

JEANNE: I just don't think we can't go around picking on foreigners just because they *are* foreigners. But it might be I'm just being naïve.

CLAUDE: I'm happy to hear that, Jeanne.

JEANNE: Maybe our boy is the patron saint of lost causes.

CLAUDE: What does that mean?

JEANNE: I just had a thought: nobody uses or takes much notice of public telephone boxes any more and nobody uses or takes much notice of crucifixes any more either. I mean, what's the point in protecting things nobody gives a damn about any more?

CLAUDE: I give a damn. It's the law. Have you got any other bullshit to tell me? Where's the corkscrew?

JEANNE: On duty?

(CLAUDE pulls out the cork)

CLAUDE: What are you waiting for ? The case is closed.

JEANNE: Closed?

CLAUDE: 'Act of vandalism – suspects unknown' – closed.

JEANNE: And now?

CLAUDE: And now – we eat!

(JEANNE isn't at all happy but she takes her place at the table)

(End of 3)

4.

One month later. Daylight in the forest. It is Sunday. CLAUDE dressed in civilian hunting uniform stands idly with his rifle in his arms. The sound of dogs and the crack of rifles can be distantly heard. CLAUDE gets out a flask of eau de vie and sips. We hear suddenly the rustling of trees and bushes. CLAUDE reacts with his rifle and is surprised to see JEANNE emerge. She too is in civilian uniform and ports a McDo cup with a straw in it. In her other hand she has a white plastic Super U bag with something heavy hidden inside.)

JEANNE: Don't shoot – it's me, Jeanne!

CLAUDE: Jesus, you scared me! We're hunting today!

JEANNE: I can see! They told me up on the road I could find you down here.

CLAUDE: I'm acting look-out – if I see or hear anything I contact the others. (He holds up his mobile phone) But what the heck could be so important that you couldn't talk to me about it when we're working together and not on my day off?

JEANNE: I wanted to see you in 'hunter' mode I suppose. You've talked about it enough. I wanted to see it with my own eyes.

CLAUDE: You should have asked earlier.

JEANNE: I wanted to surprise you.

CLAUDE: You have!

(CLAUDE nods at her McDo cup)

CLAUDE: You're letting the side down a bit there aren't you?

JEANNE: I like America.

CLAUDE: Have you ever been?

JEANNE: Not yet. But I met some in Paris. They're not like us.

CLAUDE: Luckily!

JEANNE: They're more open, more confident, more friendly.

CLAUDE: Yes and more dumb – have you heard their thick President talking recently?

JEANNE: I don't think we should tarnish an entire nation just because of its thick President.

CLAUDE: Shush!

(They listen to the sounds of the distant hunt)

CLAUDE: Sorry, pet, what did you say?

JEANNE: Nothing. What news on the 'The Mystery of the Broken Crucifix'?

CLAUDE: Action – I returned to the Hadids.

JEANNE: Again? How many times have you been there in the last month?

CLAUDE: One or two.

JEANNE: Ten by my count. It's harassment.

CLAUDE: It's the job! And thanks to my perseverance – even if you want to call it harassment – they've told me and assured me their errant son is back in Paris staying with friends, no fixed address.

JEANNE: Will you speak to the Paris police?

CLAUDE: Who cares? Our little community is safer for his absence. If he stayed, it would only have been a question of time before he tripped up anyway. The family knows we're on their case and that's the most important.

JEANNE: But it's him we're after, not the family.

CLAUDE: Reinforce the message.

JEANNE: But I don't agree with that at all!

CLAUDE: Oh, and before I forget to mention it, I haven't forgotten your Evaluation Report is due. I promise I'll finish it by the end of the week. I'm a bit slow with the key board.

JEANNE: I wanted to ask you about that.

CLAUDE: No need – you'll get a glowing report.

JEANNE: Really?

CLAUDE: Of course, you're a lovely girl, Jeanne!

JEANNE: I'm not a girl, Claude, I'm a woman and whether in your eyes I'm pretty enough, I don't really give a shit either way.

CLAUDE: Of course you're full of energy and passion and you want to change the world, I understand that! I was the same. But in the years to come you're going to be tested and it'll start with little, insignificant things like choices, questions, answers, politics – at home and at work - and so on and temptation will be with you constantly. But if you can find a way to live with all that, you'll have a great career in front of you.

(JEANNE is silent)

CLAUDE: A few years ago we had millions of them too but at least we knew where they were, where to find them. Boars. Then what happened? Democracy got soft – animal lovers and environmentalists took over at the helm - and they sensed it and left their forests and started to integrate with human habitation so now they're everywhere. They transport diseases, cause accidents and damage our crops. They take much but give back little. Our world can't go on like that. There's always a bill to pay and it's usually us dumb idiots who end up paying.

The two races can't live side by side. How can our children play safely outside when we know there is a prehistoric killer round the corner? Oh yes, it's a dangerous place is a forest ! Like a jungle – on the surface it looks so lush you could eat it but scratch just under the surface and you see the terror hiding in the undergrowth. They're not like us – they're not open, free or tolerant. But us, we can teach them these things.

JEANNE: And are they going to put the cross back up?

CLAUDE: There are rumours they're going to erect it closer to the church and where it used to be they want to put up a 'Welcome to the Village' sign in five different languages.

JEANNE: Will Arabic be one of the languages?

CLAUDE: You'll have to ask Jeanne-Christophe about that – it's his idea.

JEANNE: I've written a resignation letter, Claude.

CLAUDE: Eh?

JEANNE: I said 'I've written a resignation letter'

(CLAUDE studies JEANNE, not sure if she's joking)

CLAUDE: Resignation? You want to quit the force?

JEANNE: You're putting words into my mouth, Claude. I did a lot of thinking and soul-searching and discussing with the help of my 'husband' and I've decided to ask for a transfer to Nantes. I don't want to continue my training here, not like . . . this.

I joined up because I want to make the world a better, safer place. I know its sound so naive and stupid but that's what I think. I think to want to do that, make the world a safer place, carries with it a certain kind of nobility. And then I met you and you asked me to look and listen, so I looked and listened and decided I didn't like what I saw and heard.

You're part of this village, Claude, I see that now. But the Law is bigger than you and this little place and if I don't seek to maintain the nobility and dignity of that service, I'm lost. So you see I've had a difficult choice to make: end up like you or just be 'me'?

CLAUDE: And?

(JEANNE opens her white plastic bag and brings out an axe which she offers to CLAUDE by the head so he can take it correctly by the handle)

JEANNE: Same blade, same size, same traces. I couldn't work it out – who could be so much a part of the landscape that no one in a million years would ever guess he would have done such a thing? I tried to put the idea out of my head and even tried to transfer the poor old Hadids into the scenario you suggested but after all those conversations we shared I put two and two together and got four.

CLAUDE: You're hiding something. What are you hiding?

JEANNE: I said I wrote a resignation letter. I didn't say if I sent it or not.

CLAUDE: Do what you want. I'm not bothered about you. I'm bothered about me and against me you have no proof.

JEANNE: I know and you know it as well and we're the only two people in the world who do know it. But that's my dilemma, Claude - 'selective policing' as you call it. It'll be your word against mine and who will they believe: a young recruit or a twenty-year old veteran?

(CLAUDE thinks)

CLAUDE: I couldn't do it in one go – too risky. I kept the axe in the boot of the car and gave it a whack every now and then if I was passing, sometimes once a week, sometimes twice. It took six months in total. I'm surprised I got away with it for as long and nobody noticed.

Not much happens here, Jeanne, and that's the way I like it.

JEANNE: This never had anything to do with the Muslim kid who ran off to Paris.

CLAUDE: No, not really.

JEANNE: But you cut down a crucifix?

CLAUDE: If there's no crime, Jeanne, there's no need of cops.

JEANNE: But you cut down a crucifix??

CLAUDE: To achieve a certain end, yes.

JEANNE: I don't know whether to laugh or cry right now. Oh my poor, poor Claude, how I pity you.

(CLAUDE returns the axe to JEANNE)

CLAUDE: Save your pity. What are you going to do?

JEANNE: I haven't finished yet.

CLAUDE: There's more?

JEANNE: The Moral Lesson - the kick in the teeth.

(She takes out her wallet and unzips a hidden compartment)

JEANNE: You've asked me why I don't carry a photo of my husband around with me. Well, I do. But I don't share it with everyone in order to protect her.

CLAUDE: Her?

(She gives a photo to him. He looks at it.)

CLAUDE: Who's this, your sister?

JEANNE: My 'husband' Pierrette also known as Pierre.

CLAUDE: Ah! You drink from the furry cup? So what?

(CLAUDE returns the photo, unphased)

JEANNE: I haven't finished.

(JEANNE shows him another photo. He looks.)

CLAUDE: Who's this, Doctor Mengele and his African whore?

JEANNE: Those are my parents, Claude. My Dad, on the left, was a Doctor and my mother on the right was his nurse. They met in Ghana.

(CLAUDE looks oddly from the photo to JEANNE)

JEANNE: I'm mixed race, even if I am all white. My big brother Michael is the colour of caramel.

CLAUDE: Is that my moral lesson?

JEANNE: Yes that's your moral lesson – humiliation of your conscience in front of me and every other resident of our jungle too afraid to speak out because of people like you – exceptions but not the rules.

CLAUDE: So what are you going to do now?

JEANNE: It's not what I'm going to do, Claude.

CLAUDE: Me? I'm not doing or saying anything. The next act or word that comes out of you is the total responsibility of our own conscience. You're writing this story, Jeanne – I'm just reacting to it.

(JEANNE puts the bag with the axe in it down on the ground and turns to go. Just then CLAUDE's phone beeps.)

CLAUDE: He's on his way, our little prehistoric immigrant – watch your step!

(JEANNE stops but doesn't turn)

CLAUDE: There's too much importance placed on words today! 'Queer or straight', 'retarded or normal', 'Rosbif or Yankee', 'Honky or nigger'! What the fuck is a word?

(JEANNE rushes to CLAUDE, snatches the rifle from him and verbally explodes in his face)

JEANNE: It's a fucking *lot* is a word!

(We see CLAUDE unmasked by a young woman with principles he has long lost. She hands him back the rifle but he lets it fall to the ground along with himself. JEANNE turns with dignity and walks away from CLAUDE yet again. We hear the hunting dogs getting closer.)

CLAUDE: Jeanne ! *JEANNE !*

(JEANNE stops and turns to look again at CLAUDE)

CLAUDE: Did you send it, your resignation letter?

(JEANNE looks at him for a moment and then slowly, calculatingly, retraces her steps, bends down to be at the same level as him, looks into his eyes for a moment and says : . . .)

JEANNE: Guess.

(A brief pause then cut to black. End of play.)

www.ingramcontent.com/pod-product-compliance
Lightning Source LLC
Chambersburg PA
CBHW071423180526
45170CB00001B/197